996

Bellwood, Peter S

The Polynesians

# The
# POLYNESIANS

*For Teremoana*

Peter Bellwood

# The POLYNESIANS
## Prehistory of an island people

WITH 107 ILLUSTRATIONS

THAMES AND HUDSON

*996*

*Ancient Peoples and Places*

GENERAL EDITOR: GLYN DANIEL

© *1978 Thames and Hudson Ltd, London*

*Library of Congress Catalog card number 78-55086*

*Printed in Great Britain by*
*BAS Printers Limited, Over Wallop, Hampshire*

# Contents

# 1
# Introduction

'It is extraordinary that the same Nation should have spread themselves over all the isles in this vast Ocean from New Zealand to this Island which is almost a fourth part of the circumference of the Globe.'

Captain James Cook at Easter Island, March 1774.

As a distinct human population, characterized by unified origins and close ethnic homogeneity, the Polynesians were the most widely spread people on earth prior to AD 1500. They alone settled the islands that we now call Polynesia, situated within the vast triangle formed by the Hawaiian Islands, Easter Island and New Zealand. With sides approximating 6500 kilometres in length this triangle covers almost twice the area of the continental USA, although the actual ratio of sea to land is in the vicinity of seventy to one. The Polynesians began their expansion into this previously uninhabited zone soon after 2000 BC, and they had settled all major islands, including New Zealand, by AD 1000.

In the annals of ethnography the Polynesians occupy a rather special place. Their voyaging skills, their rich oral traditions, and their colourful and often despotic chiefdoms have interested outsiders since the days of Captain Cook. Many of the great museums of the world have splendid displays of Polynesian arts and handicrafts, and I think few would dispute the sheer mastery of form and style which some of these objects show. The Polynesians had no metals, and they ceased to make pottery about 1500 years ago. However, their wood-carvings, their stone adzes and their shell fishhooks were all manufactured according to high standards of craftsmanship, and the field archaeologist has the added interest of a wide range of stone monuments, of which those on Easter Island are perhaps the most famous.

Over the past twenty years a good deal of archaeology has been carried out in the area, and the results of this work form the core of this book. My interests are the prehistory of the islands, which I terminate for convenience around AD 1800.

1

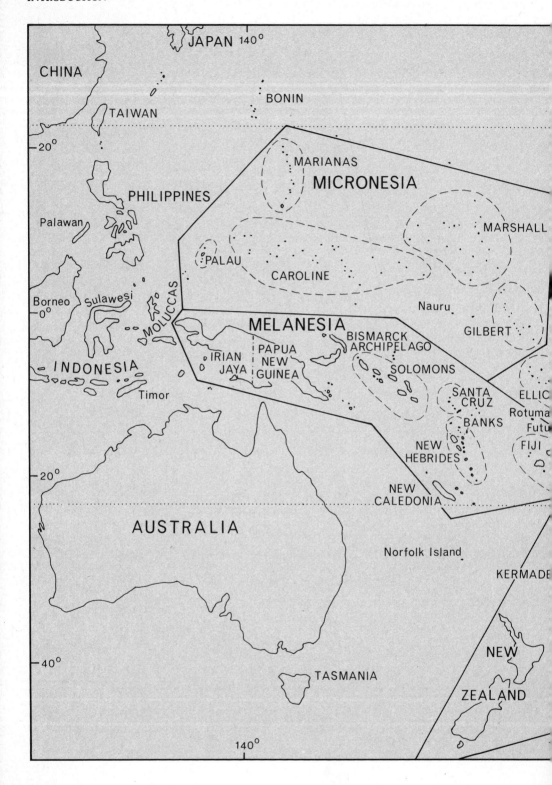

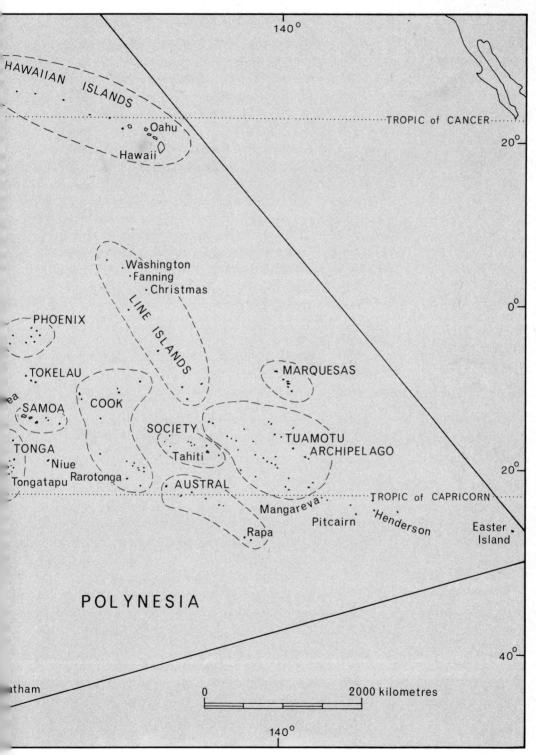

140°

TROPIC of CANCER

20°

Oahu

Hawaii

.Washington
·Fanning
·Christmas

0°

LINE ISLANDS

PHOENIX

.TOKELAU

MARQUESAS

ea

SAMOA

COOK

SOCIETY

TUAMOTU
ARCHIPELAGO

TONGA

Tahiti

·Niue

Tongatapu

Rarotonga

AUSTRAL

20°

Mangareva

TROPIC of CAPRICORN

Rapa

Pitcairn

Henderson

Easter
Island

POLYNESIA

40°

atham

0          2000 kilometres

140°

1 The Pacific Ocean and its main cultural divisions.

## The geography of Polynesia[1]

Polynesia forms the largest geographical subdivision of the world's largest ocean – the Pacific, 20,000 kilometres wide between Singapore and Panama. While the greater part of this ocean is empty of land, it does support a very large number of islands stretching in tropical latitudes from the coasts of South-East Asia to as far as Easter Island. Beyond Easter Island lie an empty 4000 kilometres stretching to the South American coast.

The islands form, therefore, a long, thick belt which gradually tapers away in the east. In the far west lie the archipelagos of the Philippines and Indonesia – large, close-set islands constructed for the most part on shallow shelves extending out from the Asian continent. Despite its fragmented appearance, Indonesia is today one of the world's largest nations, both in area and in population, and, together with the Philippines, it may have been the home of the ultimate ancestors of the Polynesians some 5000 years ago. To the east of Indonesia lie the Melanesian islands – again large and close-set, and comprising New Guinea, the Bismarcks, Solomons, New Hebrides, New Caledonia and Fiji.

All these westerly archipelagos have in common the presence of mixed rock types similar to those of the adjacent continents of

2 The island of Moorea, Society Islands, with its lagoon and barrier reef.

Asia and Australia, and they have been subjected to similar processes of folding and faulting. This zone is also part of a belt of seismic instability extending around the Pacific rim, and earthquakes and explosive volcanic eruptions are frequently recorded (the famous volcano of Krakatoa lies between Java and Sumatra). The islands of Polynesia and Micronesia are, on the other hand, of totally different formation, although New Zealand, Tonga, and some of the western Micronesian islands do belong geologically with the western continental group.

The oceanic islands of Polynesia (excluding New Zealand and Tonga) are generally formed of basaltic rocks extruded from ancient volcanoes, and only on the island of Hawaii is there active vulcanicity at present; the craters of Mauna Loa and Kilauea are always at least gently active, but their lavas do not create the violent eruptions that occur so often on the Pacific rim. The Polynesian islands generally lack sedimentary rocks, apart from recent alluvial deposits, and they are also much smaller and more

3 A village and bay inside an extinct volcanic crater; Apolima Island, Western Samoa.

widespread than the islands of Melanesia. This circumstance of course made their settlement by prehistoric voyagers much more difficult.

The islands of Polynesia form a number of major groups, with isolated islands dotted here and there between them. The main groups in the west are the Tongan, Samoan and Ellice groups. The Cook, Society and Austral groups occupy the centre, and the Marquesas and Tuamotus the east, with Easter Island as a far-off isolate. The Hawaiian Islands and New Zealand are separated to north and south respectively of the main west-east belt, and their settlements obviously required major feats of navigation on the part of the Polynesians.

The best known of the Polynesian islands are the high volcanic formations with their jagged profiles, deep gorge-like valleys and cascading waterfalls. The Society, Hawaiian and Samoan Islands are mainly in this category, and the former are renowned for 2, 3 their natural beauty, having the added attractions of barrier reefs and gentle enclosed lagoons. Some of the high islands lack barrier reefs, and this is the case with the very rugged Marquesas, and also with the Hawaiian Islands.

The atolls provide an ecological pole to the verdant high islands, and comprise thin strips of coral arranged like a necklace around a central lagoon. They are the products of living coral reefs which have survived and grown since the submergence of a volcanic island to which they were originally attached, and because the resulting coral strips are only raised a few metres above sea-level these islands are very prone to hurricane devastation. They also lack soil and surface water, and are generally very poor environments for unequipped human settlement, despite their well-stocked lagoons. There are quite a 4 number of atolls in Polynesia, particularly in the northern Cook and Tuamotu Islands, and they are generally very small in land area. The Tuamotus actually comprise 75 separate atolls, but total only 800 square kilometres of land. Micronesia is the atoll region *par excellence*, and the many islands of the Carolines, Marshalls and Gilberts are almost entirely of this form.

Between the high islands and the atolls there are a number of intermediate island types, such as raised atolls, or volcanic islands with raised barrier reefs. New Zealand, being larger than the rest of Polynesia put together, will be given special consideration later on. For the moment, these environmental descriptions will be concerned only with the small tropical islands.

Climatically, the Polynesian islands are tropical, only Rapa and Easter Island being any distance below the Tropic of Capricorn. They all have hot and fairly wet climates, with rainfall peaks generally coming between December and February (the southern summer). There is a belt of low rainfall in the eastern Pacific, running along the Equator, but none of the major group except the Marquesas fall in this belt, and it is of little significance for our purposes. Elsewhere in Polynesia, rainfall generally exceeds 1500 mm per annum. Occasional summer hurricanes also penetrate the region from the west, and these often cause severe devastation.

From the viewpoint of the travelling Polynesian, the prevailing directions of winds and currents would clearly be of great importance. It is therefore of considerable interest to note that these trend from east to west for most of the year. The trade winds blow from a general easterly direction for most months, but may be replaced by occasional westerlies during the summer. Ocean currents also flow from east to west, except for a rather narrow west–east flowing countercurrent in the general vicinity of the Equator. This means that a drifting canoe in Polynesia will tend to move from east to west, and records of past drift voyages,[2] together with a more recent computer experiment,[3]

4 The lagoon of Penrhyn atoll, northern Cook Islands.

have shown this to be the case. In fact, the Polynesians probably had to sail quite hard into the wind to discover many of their islands.

In terms of indigenous resources, the Polynesian islands would have been poorly equipped to support newly arrived human populations. All the major food plants and animals were introduced into Polynesia by man, and of truly indigenous plants, only a few nuts, fruits and fibre-producing plants ever acquired much importance. So the mainstays of Polynesian life – coconut, taro, yam, banana, breadfruit, and the food animals (pig, dog and chicken) – were clearly transported intentionally by early navigators. Fish were obviously an exception, and in New Zealand the earliest settlers were also confronted with a large edible avifauna, but this was soon reduced to virtual extinction.

## European navigators in Polynesia[4]

A brief survey of Polynesia's role in European navigational history will lead into the final historical section of this introduction. Strangely enough, it took European ships over 300 years to 'discover' the whole of Polynesia – a procedure which began with Ferdinand Magellan in 1521 and which finally ended in 1835. We are in fact closer in time to Captain Cook, the greatest of the Pacific explorers (between 1769 and 1778), than Cook was to Magellan!

Between 1521 and 1767, the history of exploration in the Pacific was one of rather hit-and-miss adventurism. The Spanish were interested mainly in sailing from South America to the Philippines, and their routes of travel were generally north of the main Polynesian groups. The Dutch also made a few sporadic forays, but between 1521 and 1767 major discoveries were very few. Magellan passed through the northern Tuamotus on his voyage round the world, and Mendaña discovered the Marquesas in 1595. Tasman (a Dutchman) paused briefly off New Zealand in 1642, and his countryman Roggeveen stopped at Easter Island in 1722. None of these early discoveries produced much anthropological information, and the first reports of mature scientific value came with the exploring expeditions of British and French navigators in the later eighteenth century.

It is from the period between 1760 and 1800 that we have our most valuable records about ancient Polynesian societies. The exploring expeditions of this period were well equipped to make scientific observations, and many carried professional scientists and artists. The more famous of these expeditions were led by Englishmen such as Cook, Wallis and Bligh, and by Frenchmen such as Bougainville, La Pérouse, and de Surville. These men beheld a traditional Polynesia which will never be seen again; by the turn of the nineteenth century Polynesian societies, particularly in the larger groups such as the Societies and Hawaii, were undergoing unprecedented upheavals. European artefacts and guns, introduced diseases, and a rather unbridled desire to exploit soon reduced Polynesian society and population to a shadow of its former self. And in the wake of the explorers came the seedier elements of European society – whalers, beachcombers, and finally slavers.

In Cook's day the Polynesians were regarded by some philosophers and scientists as noble savages, survivors of a lost Golden Age. James Cook himself was clearer-headed than this, and was indeed a rare pillar of common sense for his time. This is why his journals, together with those of his colleague Joseph Banks, are the most important ever written on Polynesian societies.[5] He was not motivated by personal greed or religious belief, or by armchair romanticism. However, after his untimely death on the island of Hawaii in 1778, Polynesian fortunes declined rapidly. Polynesian-European relations inevitably worsened, and the acquisition of guns by Polynesians led to a frightful escalation of local warfare, particularly in New Zealand. Although royal dynasties eventually established control in Tonga, Hawaii and the Societies, they were unable to stem the tide of change. By the early 1800s missionaries were spreading rapidly throughout the area, converting people who were now regarded as benighted, and certainly not noble, savages. The old respect for Polynesian culture had gone, and the missionaries, with an unusual mixture of gentleness and repression, had created a bewildered and somewhat ashamed Polynesia by the later nineteenth century. Although it is now rather fashionable to blame missionaries for the almost total destruction of Polynesian society, I would say in their favour that they did preserve many things, particularly land, in the hands of the Polynesians themselves. Regarded in hindsight, the bans on singing and dancing and the enforced wearing of European-style clothing are really rather trivial. For if the commercial enterprises of the Victorian era had had their way, there could well be nothing left of Polynesia at all. As Sterndale wrote of the Cook Islands in 1874:[6]

In presence of the increasing interest of commercial men which is now being directed to the South Pacific, and the rapid decay of the aborigines, the period at which they [i.e. the Cook Islands] shall pass into the possession of Europeans has simply become a question of time.

The Polynesians, of course, did not die out. From the nadir of the nineteenth century they have risen again, and there are now conscious attempts to blend the new and the traditional into a modern Polynesian way of life, lived among a number of independent or prospectively independent island states. Increasing populations and an awareness of human rights are now a part of Polynesia, and the future may turn out to be just as interesting as the past.

## The whence of the Polynesians – theories before 1952[7]

James Cook and his contemporaries were to the Polynesians as the Roman authors were to the Celts. They recorded many vital things which we could never otherwise have recovered today, despite the growth of scientific investigation. Unfortunately, they were not trained anthropologists, and they had difficulties in understanding local languages, although Cook managed remarkably well in this regard. Nevertheless, none of them ever sat down with a group of Polynesians and tried to record a full set of origin traditions. That they did not do so is a great loss to science.

In the late eighteenth century there was some reticence about speculating too far on Polynesian origins. The prevailing opinion was that the Polynesians came from the west, and that they were related to the peoples of Micronesia, Indonesia and the Philippines, but not Melanesia or Australia. This view has turned out to be quite correct in the light of modern knowledge, but the detailed knowledge which we have now has only emerged after 150 years of confused theorizing. Without the modern disciplines of archaeology and comparative linguistics we would still be wallowing in confusion.

In the nineteenth century the only sources available to those interested in Polynesian origins were some rather vague observations on racial type, languages, comparative ethnology, and traditions. The last-named were not collected systematically until after 1850 in most regions, and by this time they were of course subject to untold degrees of contamination, although many traditions contain undoubted historical truth. In the earlier years of the century the Polynesians were variously traced to India, the Americas, or even to a sunken continent in the middle of the Pacific. In the later years the emphasis was placed much more on the traditions, which were now being collected rather avidly on the assumption that the Polynesians were dying out.

Among the more outstanding writers of the nineteenth century we could list Horatio Hale,[8] an American who in 1846 suggested on linguistic and traditional grounds that the Polynesians came from the Moluccas, and from there settled Polynesia via Fiji, Tonga and Samoa. In this over-all sense Hale was fairly correct in his interpretations, although many of his details are understandably awry. Following Hale, we have a very prolific writer, S. Percy Smith,[9] who published his views on Polynesian origins in 1898–9. Smith depended almost entirely on traditions, collected mainly from Rarotonga, and derived the Polynesians ultimately from India, via Indonesia and Fiji, whence they arrived in Tonga and Samoa about AD 450. A slightly different stream from Fiji then settled the rest of Polynesia between 650 and 900. These later dates are indeed very reasonable, although we now know that Tonga and Samoa were settled by 1000 BC, and we also know that the Polynesians were not Caucasoids derived from India. Many scholars today dispute the value of traditions, especially as used by men like Smith, although I believe that he did create quite a useful historical narrative. The problem with the great morass of recorded tradition is in distinguishing what is true from what is false, and indeed we shall never know this for certain, since the story-tellers are all long dead.

One impression that does come from most nineteenth-century works is that the Polynesians were regarded as a single racial group, even if there were those who proposed more than one stream. After 1895, even this morsel of good sense was partially abandoned, and for fifty years the game of Polynesian origin-tracing reached a rather low level. The idea that the Polynesians were the results of mixture between several layers of different ethnic and racial origin now took firm root. The main problem was that no two scholars could agree on the order of composition of the layers.

The racial strata put forward at this time were loosely grouped under the headings of Negroid, Caucasoid and Mongoloid. It is unnecessary to give details, apart from mentioning the names of John Fraser, J. Macmillan Brown, R. Sullivan, Ralph Linton and E. S. C. Handy, all of whom published their theories between 1895 and 1930. At the same time a number of other scholars maintained the idea of the Polynesians as being one racial group, but perhaps in more than one stratum. This was of course Smith's theory, and it was also developed by Churchill and Williamson. To some extent these theories were based on the view that cultures could travel across the Pacific like sealed bottles, unchanged until they settled down in various islands where they either influenced or were influenced by cultures already there. A good example of this is Handy's scheme:[10] he identified two strata in Polynesia, the first being of Vedic, Hindu and South-East Asian origin, the second being of south Chinese Buddhist origin. He believed that the latter group established themselves as chiefs in Samoa, the Society Islands and Hawaii, and he even believed that everyday artefacts could be associated with one of the two strata. One of the soundest attacks against this argument was by the social anthropologist Ralph Piddington, who strongly advocated in 1939 what we would now regard as a more modern common-sense view.[11]

The period after 1939 is an important one for us, since common sense did prevail to an extent, and many of the theories published are still in use today. Sir Peter Buck's major work of 1944[12] derived the Polynesians as a single group through Micronesia, and he wisely avoided discussion of ultimate origins. His early settlers reached all of Polynesia except Easter Island, and some of them developed a highly ranked priestly society on the island of Raiatea in the Society group. These Raiateans were then able to influence the rest of Polynesia, including Easter Island, but excluding Tonga and Samoa, through a series of major migrations between the twelfth and the fourteenth centuries. Buck, one of the most famous Polynesian scholars and part-Maori himself, was well aware that the societies of Tonga and Samoa had evolved on slightly different lines from those in the rest of Polynesia, and these differences had in fact been clearly brought out by Edwin Burrows in 1938. I shall be returning to Burrows's analysis at the end of this chapter.

The period after the Second World War has seen a great increase in the pace of Polynesian research, mainly through the introduction of archaeology and modern linguistic techniques. The older sources such as traditions, comparative ethnology and craniology have now almost entirely given way to these new techniques, and the rate of progress in understanding the Polynesian past has been remarkable. The results of the post-war period naturally form the basis for the following chapters, and need not be discussed here. There is, however, one other recent theory about the Polynesians which has gained world-wide fame, and in which many still believe. I must state at the outset that there is no longer any reason to derive the Polynesians from the Americas, although the idea goes back well into the nineteenth century. It was resurrected in a dramatic way by Thor Heyerdahl in 1947.

In that year Heyerdahl and his companions constructed a balsa raft which they called the *Kon-Tiki*, and set out from Callao to show that South American Indians could have settled Polynesia by following the prevailing winds and currents. They had to be towed 80 kilometres offshore, since, although the prevailing currents trend from east to west, they do not commence until at least this distance away from the Peruvian coast. After sailing with winds and currents for 101 days they crash-landed on the atoll of Raroia in the Tuamotus, and thus showed that South American Indians could indeed have reached Polynesia.[13] No one would dispute this point today, but it is clearly a very different matter to say that the Polynesians themselves actually came from America. Heyerdahl elaborated this theory in his major work of 1952.[14]

To begin with, Heyerdahl was unable to accept that the Polynesians had migrated through Melanesia because of racial differences, and he believed that the Polynesian languages were unrelated to Malay. He also believed that the Polynesians had only migrated within the past 1000 years, and he ruled out South-East Asia partly on the grounds that Sanskrit words (present in Indonesian languages since before AD 500) were absent in Polynesia. He was therefore obliged to look to America, for which he already had a clear preference on ethnological grounds. He believed that Polynesia was first settled by Caucasoids from the area of Tiahuanaco in Bolivia, ultimately perhaps of North African origin. These people moved into the Pacific around AD 800, and then the true Polynesians moved down from British Columbia between 1100 and 1300, settling among the earlier Caucasoids and gradually replacing them. Heyerdahl was prepared to accept an ultimate South-East Asian origin for these Polynesians, but not a direct derivation. Naturally, many scholars resisted the idea of a South American substratum with objections which are as strong now as they were

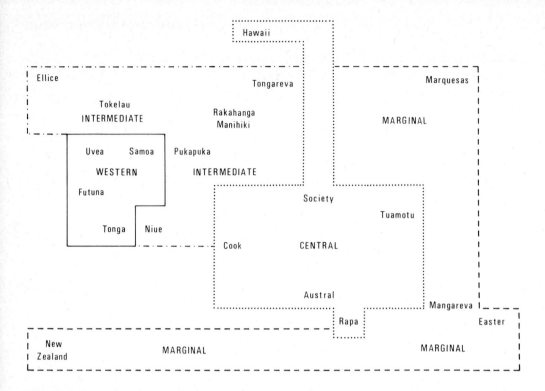

| | Hawaii | | |
|---|---|---|---|
| Ellice | Tongareva | | Marquesas |
| Tokelau INTERMEDIATE | Rakahanga Manihiki | | MARGINAL |
| Uvea  Samoa  WESTERN  Futuna | Pukapuka INTERMEDIATE | | |
| Tonga  Niue | Society | Tuamotu | |
| | Cook  CENTRAL | | |
| | Austral | | Mangareva |
| | Rapa | | Easter |
| New Zealand  MARGINAL | | | MARGINAL |

5 Polynesian cultural divisions according to Burrows. The central and marginal divisions are grouped as eastern Polynesia in this book. In the intermediate division, the atolls of Tongareva, Manihiki and Rakahanga belong to eastern Polynesia, the others to western Polynesia.

in the 1950s. The inexorable progress of research has rendered the whole framework untenable, although there are nevertheless many parallels between Polynesians and British Columbian Indians which will one day require explanation. It will be necessary to return to the work of Heyerdahl again when we come to Easter Island, for, despite his basic stance, he has in fact made some very significant contributions to Polynesian archaeology.

The modern opinion on the Polynesians is that they derive from somewhere in eastern Indonesia or the Philippines, and that they migrated through Melanesia into Polynesia between 2000 and 1000 BC. This view is soundly supported by archaeology and linguistics, although there are still a few scholars who would like to derive the Polynesians through Micronesia rather than Melanesia. Some centre ground between these two views will undoubtedly be found in the near future, now that the over-all picture is solidly and reliably established. We shall return to this topic in Chapter 3.

## Cultural divisions within Polynesia

The work by Edwin Burrows[15] mentioned above established a very significant cultural division within Polynesia. After

examining the distributions of various cultural traits, he defined 5
two major culture areas – western Polynesia and central-
marginal Polynesia. Western Polynesia comprises Tonga,
Samoa, and adjacent groups; central Polynesia includes the
Hawaiian, Society, southern Cook, Austral and Tuamotu
Islands, and marginal Polynesia includes the Marquesas, Easter
Island and New Zealand. Today, Burrows's scheme has been
modified slightly, and modern archaeologists use the term
'eastern Polynesia' to include the central and marginal divisions
shown on figure 5. The basic implication of this division is that
the two areas have undergone rather separate sequences of
development; for instance, several culture traits present widely
in eastern Polynesia, such as tanged adzes, simple shell bait-
hooks for fishing, stone food pounders, and human figures
carved in stone or wood, were virtually absent in western
Polynesia. The two regions also had contrasting techniques of
bark-cloth manufacture, house and temple building, canoe
building, kinship terminology and religion. These differences

6 The Polynesian outliers.

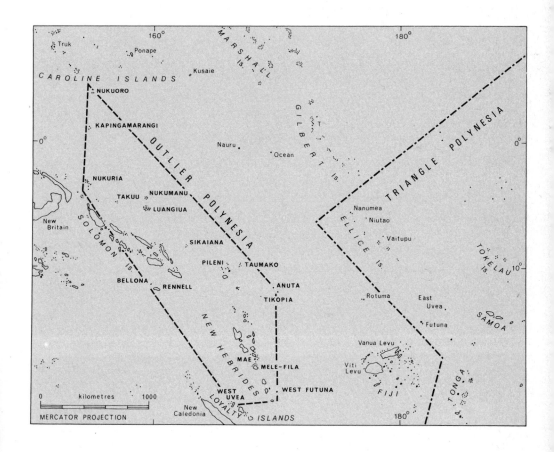

imply that the islands within each of the two divisions have shared in common certain developments, through either common inheritance or borrowing. The division is therefore quite fundamental in Polynesian culture history.

There are two other divisions of a purely geographical nature which also deserve comment. The Polynesian triangle has its apices in New Zealand, Easter Island and Hawaii (as shown in figure 1); this is Polynesia *per se*. However, there are long-established Polynesian communities (as defined linguistically) on nineteen small islands and atolls in Melanesia, most often to the east (windward) of the series of large islands forming the Solomon and New Hebrides chains, as well as New Caledonia. These are called the Polynesian outliers,[16] and in cultural terms they belong to western Polynesia.

These four terms – western, eastern, triangle and outlier Polynesia – are introduced here because they will be used again throughout this book. The reader should acquaint himself with the locations of specific groups in figures 1 and 5, otherwise some confusion might arise.

# The Polynesian peoples and their cultures

The accounts provided by European explorers in the Pacific enable us to give a fairly full description of the Polynesians and their society in the late eighteenth century. Indeed, many aspects of prehistoric Polynesian life still survive today, and this is particularly true of the languages. The peoples themselves have changed through intermarriage with outsiders, and their cultures have of course adapted in many ways to the modern world to which they now belong. Nevertheless, Polynesia still retains much of the allure and charm which first attracted Europeans two hundred years ago.

## The Polynesian people

Recent archaeological work has shown that New Guinea and Australia were settled by 30–40,000 years ago, almost certainly by dark-skinned Australoid[1] populations ancestral to the present Melanesians and Australian Aborigines. The islands of the Philippines and Indonesia were also once settled by these Australoids, and in western Indonesia they may well have a very long ancestry going back to the times of *Homo erectus*, over one million years ago. The Australoids are in fact the true indigenes of Indonesia and the western Pacific, and until some 7000 years ago the islands east of the Bismarck Archipelago, or perhaps even east of New Guinea itself, were quite possibly uninhabited (see below).

The Polynesians are members of the Mongoloid division of mankind,[2] and as such have an ultimate origin rather separate from the Australoids. The Mongoloids may have been expanding from the South-East Asian mainland into Indonesia throughout the Holocene epoch; the majority of Indonesians and Filipinos are certainly Mongoloids today, although there are isolated populations in these countries who do preserve traces of a much more ancient Australoid heritage. This is especially true

7 A Samoan family,
photographed *c*.1900 by
Charles Kerry of Sydney.

of the Negritos of Malaya, the Andaman Islands, and the
Philippines. There is a small amount of skeletal evidence from
Indonesia and the Philippines which also supports this
hypothesis of recent Mongoloid expansion.

By about 3000 BC some of these Mongoloid peoples began to
expand into Melanesia. At the present state of research it is
uncertain whether the Australoid populations of Melanesia had
already occupied the islands beyond New Guinea to as far as the
New Hebrides and New Caledonia, although I strongly suspect
this to be the case. Most of the Melanesians show few traces of
any substantial intermarriage with Mongoloids, and this may be
because they had already settled their islands, with the exception
of Fiji, with quite large populations who were able to resist a high
degree of Mongoloid genetic influence. Nevertheless, certain
populations in coastal Papua New Guinea and the New Hebrides
do have what appear to be a higher proportion of Polynesian
characteristics, and the over-all situation was certainly more
complicated than can be indicated here.

8 Rangui, a Maori chief, drawn by L. de Sainson on the voyage of the *Astrolabe*, under the command of Dumont d'Urville, 1826–9.

The Polynesians themselves were also affected by inter-marriage with Melanesians, and this has led to several changes in physical characteristics away from South-East Asian norms. The Polynesians, as well as many Melanesians, are quite tall (averaging 169–173 cm for males) and heavily built. The Mongoloid traits of light skin, straight black hair, relative scarcity of body hair, and fairly high frequencies of shovel-shaped incisor teeth and the epicanthic (or Mongoloid) eyefold are all well marked in Polynesians, but there are many individuals with darker skins and wavy or curly hair who approximate more to the Melanesian phenotype. In an average Polynesian village one would see a range of phenotypes from strongly Mongoloid to partly Melanesian, although today the picture is somewhat masked by 200 years of intermarriage with Europeans and other outsiders.

It should also be added that the Polynesians do resemble in appearance the South American Indians, because the latter are also Mongoloids of ultimate East Asian derivation. While it was

7

8

once thought that certain blood-group percentages could indicate a direct connection between American Indians and Polynesians, this is no longer an acceptable argument.[3] Furthermore, there is no proof that Polynesians have any Caucasoid ancestry, despite the popularity of this theory many years ago. The theory of Thor Heyerdahl, described in Chapter 1, thus no longer has support from physical anthropology, and Robert Langdon has more recently produced an equally intriguing but insupportable theory that many of the Polynesians are of Basque ancestry.[4]

It is unfortunate that there is as yet no full skeletal record to document the ancestry of the Polynesians, for the necessary materials have not so far turned up from sites dating prior to 1000 years ago. Most of the analyses carried out by physical anthropologists and geneticists have therefore been based on living populations, although there are quite large museum collections of cranial material which are certainly prehistoric. Some of these have been analysed by Michael Pietrusewsky[5] of the University of Hawaii, and he has divided them by computer techniques into three groups, the first being from Tonga and Samoa, and taking in Fiji in eastern Melanesia. The second group includes the Society and Tuamotu Islands. The third includes many of the peripheral islands of Polynesia, such as New Zealand, Hawaii, and Easter Island. The first two groups probably reflect a good deal of recent intermarriage, since this is well attested historically and traditionally. The third group may consist of isolated islands which have preserved in common many aspects of an early Polynesian phenotype. Perhaps the most likely conclusion for the Polynesians is that they stem from an initially small and somewhat homogeneous population, which entered the area through Fiji. The subsequent three millennia of relative isolation have led to a degree of genetic differentiation which is recognizable, if slight. As a group, the Polynesians are very much more homogeneous than the Melanesians, and their racial history within Polynesia has covered only a relatively short space of time.

## Polynesian linguistic history

The same conclusion about homogeneity can be drawn from linguistics. The Polynesians speak about thirty closely related languages which form one branch of a very widespread family known as Austronesian. In late prehistoric times each group of islands had a single major language, with dialect differences in some, such as the Marquesas, New Zealand and the southern Cooks. The total population of Polynesian-speakers prior to 1770 may have been between 300,000 and 400,000, although estimates of prehistoric population size do vary considerably.

The Austronesian languages as a whole number between 700 and 800, and are spoken throughout Indonesia, the Philippines, Micronesia, Polynesia, Madagascar, and parts of South Vietnam and Malaya.[6] They are also spoken widely in the islands of Melanesia, but the languages of most of New Guinea, large parts of the Solomons, and the whole of Australia are totally unrelated to Austronesian, and probably go back to the first Australoid settlers of these areas more than 30,000 years ago. However, it should not be assumed that the Austronesian languages correlate precisely with Mongoloid populations, and the other non-Austronesian languages with Australoids; nothing could be further from the truth in Melanesia, and as we have noted above these people are basically Australoid rather than Mongoloid in ultimate origin. The early period of Austronesian expansion is a complex one, and in over-all terms the Polynesians are a relatively minor side-branch.

The Austronesians have thus spread themselves well over half-way round the world, and they had completed this achievement by about AD 500. From linguistic reconstructions it is now clear that they began their expansion between 5000 and 7000 years ago from the general region of Taiwan, the Philippines and Indonesia; they could possibly have an original homeland somewhere in the region of southern China, but this is at present beyond the range of linguistic reconstruction and merely hypothesis. From reconstructions of the vocabulary of the earliest Austronesian languages it is possible to say that cultivated taro, yams, banana, breadfruit, coconut and probably rice were being grown in Island South-East Asia by 3000 BC, and pigs and perhaps dogs were present too. Material culture included pottery, outrigger canoes with sails, and stone tools.[7] Recent archaeology in South-East Asia has demonstrated the accuracy of some parts of this purely linguistic reconstruction, and this is of some importance because it is from this cultural milieu that the Polynesians originated. They entered the Pacific as neolithic horticulturists and fishermen, and without their sailing canoes they could never have reached their final homes.

The languages of Polynesia actually form rather a minor branch of the whole Austronesian family, although the    9

Polynesians were undoubtedly the most widespread single group of Austronesians. Owing to a relatively short time depth of perhaps 3500 years the Polynesian languages never diverged as much as those in the islands to the west, and some of the eastern Polynesian languages preserved a high degree of mutual intelligibility until European contact.

A family tree for the Polynesian languages is set out in figure 9.[8] This figure also shows the position of Polynesian within the whole Austronesian family; it is in fact a side-branch of a major subgroup called Oceanic, which probably began to differentiate in western Melanesia before 3000 BC. Within Oceanic is a smaller subgroup called Eastern Oceanic,[9] which includes some of the Melanesian languages in the southern Solomons and central and northern New Hebrides, as well as Fijian and Polynesian. Eastern Oceanic was probably beginning to differentiate by 2000 BC. The Fijian language, like the people and culture, is the closest cousin to Polynesian within Melanesia, and Fijian and Polynesian share a common ancestral language, called Proto-Central-Pacific, which was located in Fiji at about 1500 BC.

According to linguists the first settlement in the Polynesian triangle probably took place in the Tongan Islands, and archaeology fixes the date of this settlement at 1300 BC or before. By about 1000 BC these earliest Polynesians had spread through the northern islands of the Tongan group to Samoa, and the ancestral Polynesian languages gradually underwent a major separation into the Tongic and Nuclear Polynesian subgroups. The eastern Polynesian languages relate more closely to Samoan than they do to Tongan, and are thus included with Samoan in Nuclear Polynesian. The initial settlement of eastern Polynesia, perhaps to the Marquesas or Society groups, took place early in the first millennium AD, most probably from Samoa on both archaeological and linguistic grounds. The Polynesian outliers also belong linguistically within Nuclear Polynesian,[10] and much of the original impetus for their settlement may have come from the Ellice Islands and East Futuna (Hoorn Islands). It was once thought that the Polynesian outliers were remnants of the earliest migrating Polynesians, left behind in Melanesia. This is now known to be mostly unlikely; their inhabitants have settled these islands from the east, and from ultimate sources in western Polynesia.

In eastern Polynesia it seems apparent that the Marquesas, Society Islands and Easter Island were all settled by about AD

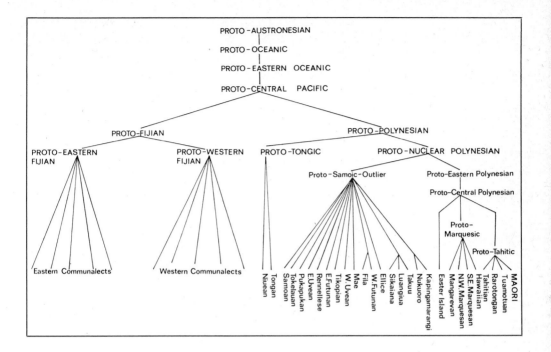

9 A family tree for the Fijian and Polynesian languages.

500, and both archaeology and linguistics are here in support. The other islands were settled mainly between AD 500 and 1000, with most of the impetus perhaps coming from the Society Islands. The languages of the Society, Cook, Austral and Tuamotu Islands and New Zealand all belong in a subgroup called Tahitic, whereas those of the Marquesas and Hawaiian Islands and Mangareva may belong to a smaller second group called Marquesic. The size and importance of the Tahitic group correlates well with traditional evidence that the Society Islands were responsible for many of the settlements in eastern Polynesia.

The vocabulary of Proto-Polynesian, spoken in western Polynesia at about 1000 BC, is of great importance, and many words have now been reconstructed by linguists.[11] The speakers had the whole range of domesticated plants and animals present in Polynesia – these will be described below – and they had outrigger canoes. They fought with bows, arrows, slings and spears; they probably built fortifications, and they built their houses and temples on raised platforms of earth or stone. Apparently they did not live in villages, and neither did most of their descendants at the time of European contact.

The importance of these reconstructions needs no emphasis. It should also be noted that Polynesian languages show no convincing evidence of substrata from South America or any other parts of the globe, and Polynesia was probably settled only once through the west, by people with a single language derived from Fiji. The present Polynesian languages have all descended from this single ancestor in ways which reflect the major trends of Polynesian culture history.

## Polynesian societies

In prehistoric times the islands of Polynesia were each divided into a number of territorial divisions; on atolls, these divisions tended to correspond to individual islets (depending on size) grouped around the lagoon; while on the high volcanic islands the divisions were generally radial and shaped like pie-segments, with extended coastal lands and boundaries tapering off in the mountainous interiors. These high island divisions thus ensured access to a stretch of coast and perhaps several valleys for their inhabitants.

Within these territories the Polynesians normally lived in scattered homesteads among plantations, with a degree of clustering around chiefly establishments. Villages and towns were generally absent, although a few unusual examples of nucleation will be given in later chapters. The territorial divisions thus defined were each the home of a tribe, and many of the larger ones were further subdivided into subtribal land divisions, which also tended to be radially arranged on high islands. Most settlement was coastal or in fertile valleys, and mountains and ridges were normally only inhabited in times of war. The tribal groups consisted of a core of resident members, both male and female, related by blood. To this core would be added a number of affines, or persons related by marriage, who would sometimes come from other tribes. In anthropological terms these tribes were not exogamous, and they were not strictly unilineal. Raymond Firth has described Polynesian descent as optative and ambilineal,[12] although a strong bias towards patrilineality and ranking by male primogeniture was clearly present.

The practical essence of this terminology is that a young man would probably inherit land and status from his father, although he could inherit from his mother if he wished – particularly if she were of high rank. In general, the status positions of chief and priest were held by males and inherited through male lines. A girl would probably reside with her husband's family on marriage, and would be unlikely to become a chief in her own right, unless she was of strong personality or if there were no other eligible contenders for the title. These statements are of course generalizations, and Polynesian societies were by no means identical. While it is impossible to describe the whole range of variation here, it might be noted that on some atolls, such as the Tokelaus, house sites and taro plots are in fact inherited matrilineally.[13] This does not necessarily mean that post-marital residence is wholly uxorilocal as well, for many Polynesian islands are so small that all cultivated lands can be reached within a few hours, and we generally find that rigid rules of post-marital residence never apply in Polynesia. The clearly defined unilineal ideologies which one finds in Melanesia are not present, and the Polynesians, like the rest of the Austronesians, probably originated from quite simple bilateral societies in Island South-East Asia.

The aspect of Polynesian social organization which excited most interest in the eighteenth century was the system of chieftainship. In the larger island groups, such as Tonga, Hawaii and the Societies, chiefs commanded powers of life and death over their subjects, and were surrounded with elaborate rituals and deferences. Brother–sister marriage is even recorded for Hawaii, to preserve the royal pedigree. The Polynesians in fact developed aristocracy to a far higher pitch than any other Pacific or South-East Asian peoples in prehistoric times, and the Hawaiians had virtually evolved a simple form of state organization – a level which they eventually reached very rapidly after acquiring European arms.

Chieftainship in Polynesia depended very much on descent. A tribal chief would theoretically descend from a line of first-born sons going back to the tribal ancestor. Lesser chiefs might descend from a younger son of the tribal ancestor, but again with mostly first-born children (sometimes including girls) in later lines. In general, a person's rank reflected his closeness to the chiefly line and the degree of primogeniture in his own lineage, and in a small ideal society every person would know his rank *vis-à-vis* every other person. Although most Polynesian societies had grown too large by European times for a total genealogical network of this kind to be remembered, such networks were certainly remembered by chiefly families, for more than 30 generations in some cases. Hence the Polynesian skill at reciting seemingly interminable genealogies – status depended upon them.

To take New Zealand as an example of a fairly traditional form of Polynesian social organization, each tribe (*iwi*) occupied, ideally, its own territory, under the leadership of a high chief (*ariki*). The tribe was further divided into smaller groups known as *hapu*; these occupied certain territories within the main tribal area, and each came under the leadership of a sub-chief (*rangatira*). The lands of the *hapu* were divided among the common people by the *rangatira*, who were in turn subject to the *ariki* in situations of tribal importance. The whole system was thus pyramidal and overlapping.

Chiefly authority was in general based on tradition, backed by the use of a good deal of force, both physical and ritual. Chiefs were imbued with a kind of supernatural aura of mystical power known as *mana*, and this could be quite dangerous to a commoner if certain precautions were not taken. The chief and his possessions were in fact *tapu*, a word which has entered English as 'taboo'. Actions which were *tapu*, and hence proscribed, included passing food over a chief's head, entering his plantations, and in Tahiti, even uttering the syllables of his name. If a Tahitian chief entered the house of a commoner, it was subsequently burnt to the ground.

Economically, chiefs acted as the kingpins of Polynesian society. They controlled land distribution, and were able to exact tribute. However, they did not amass wealth like European kings, but rather used their resources to patronize community projects, such as canoe or temple building. Polynesian chiefs were of course often ambitious, but the outlets for ambition generally took the form of territorial conquest and aggrandisement of personal status. Hence the frequent warfare characteristic of Polynesia at European contact, and the rapid rise and fall of particular local dynasties. Centralized government of any one island group was never really attained until the period of European intervention, with the exception of Tonga, where most of the group was periodically under the control of the Tui Tonga dynasty and its successors after AD 1200. However, there are other cases where unified control may have obtained in the past, and a good potential example of this is Easter Island at the peak of statue and temple construction, between AD 1100 and 1400. Unfortunately, we have no traditional accounts of this period at all, owing to the virtual demise of the population in the nineteenth century.

The most detailed recent examination of Polynesian society is that by Irving Goldman,[14] who has grouped Polynesian societies into three categories based on the degree to which ascribed status (i.e. by birth) rates against achieved status (i.e. by personal skill and ambition), and on the degree of class stratification. In his scheme, New Zealand, Tikopia, Manihiki and Rakahanga fall into a 'traditional' class, wherein status was gently graded by genealogical continua, marked class divisions were absent, and tribal territories relatively unified. The second class, of open societies, includes Easter Island, Mangaia and Niue, and in these cases the hereditary chiefs retained some traditional and religious status, whereas political power resided with a class of successful warriors who normally succeeded one another with sometimes alarming frequency. These warrior lords controlled land and distributed favours among their followers. The original tribal groups became partly dispersed through the fortunes of war, and the open societies are in fact best developed on ecologically poor islands with large populations; they represent a uniquely Polynesian experiment in the survival of the fittest.

Goldman's third group contains what he calls the 'stratified' societies; particularly Tahiti, Tonga, Mangareva and Hawaii. These societies developed quite rigidly separated chiefly and commoner classes with barriers against intermarriage, and chiefly power was particularly well advertised by a whole range of institutions, including human sacrifice. Polynesian social stratification has also been studied by Marshall Sahlins,[15] and he regards Tonga, Hawaii, Samoa and Tahiti as the most stratified, with some of the other high islands in an intermediate bracket, and the atolls, which tend to be fairly egalitarian, at the other pole. The obvious generalization which arises here is that social stratification became very marked in large volcanic islands which had both substantial and dense populations. New Zealand, with a large but scattered population, and many of the atolls, with very dense but small populations, remained relatively egalitarian, although the principles of aristocratic ranking were observed everywhere in Polynesia, and truly egalitarian societies, such as one finds in parts of the New Guinea Highlands, were absent.

Some of the better-known Polynesian societies, particularly the highly stratified ones, will be described in more detail in later chapters. The Samoans also developed an unusually elaborate council system which is rather separate from other Polynesian developments; this too will be described later.

## Polynesian economy

The economy of tropical Polynesia was based on the cultivation of a number of tubers and fruits, together with an intensive exploitation of marine resources. The major cultivated plant foods may be listed as taro, yam, sweet potato, coconut, breadfruit and banana, while lesser foods included pandanus, gourd, Tahitian chestnut, and a wide range of collected wild products. Cereals were not cultivated in Polynesia, and rice and millet, both important crops in South-East Asia, were absent. Furthermore, the only domesticated animals were the pig, dog and chicken, and these were rarely major sources of meat.

Of the plant foods, all the major ones listed above except for the sweet potato were domesticated in South-East Asia, and some possibly in New Guinea.[16] All the major ones (again with the exception of the sweet potato) are known from linguistic reconstructions to have been cultivated by the early Austronesians in Indonesia and the Philippines before 3000 BC, and reconstructions of words for gardening activities show that they were intentionally cultivated and not simply gathered wild. Archaeological evidence provides some support for this reconstruction, although most of the plants listed are soft and fibrous and have never been found to date in ancient archaeological sites. However, rice was certainly cultivated on the mainland of South-East Asia by 3500 BC, and neolithic cultures with pottery and stone adzes are found throughout most of South-East Asia by 3000 BC. Whether the South-East Asian region was indeed a very early centre of plant domestication, as some have claimed,[17] is not yet known for certain, and this is not a problem to delay us here.

Of the plants listed, the coconut certainly has the widest range of uses; it provides a solid food and a drinkable liquid, together with fibre for cordage, leaves for roofing and basketry, shells for containers, and trunks for house posts and bridges. It is tolerant of saline conditions, and is the only major cultivated plant which will grow on unmodified atolls. Its cultivated origins are unknown, but seem to lie in South-East Asia or Melanesia. The breadfruit and banana have a similar origin, and the former is a very nutritious fruit which was of great importance in the Society and Marquesas Islands. Captain Bligh of the *Bounty* was carrying breadfruit from Tahiti to the West Indies when the famous mutiny broke out in 1789.

The two major tubers of South-East Asian origin are the yams

and the taro-like plants (aroids). The yams like well-drained soil and are intolerant of very wet conditions; in fact, they were never of much importance in Polynesia outside Tonga. The aroids, on the other hand, were major staples in many islands, and flourished in man-made irrigation systems which were among the most remarkable creations of the Polynesians. The aroids belong to the family Araceae, and the major species is the taro (*Colocasia esculenta*). Irrigation systems for this plant, which

10 A wet-taro field constructed in a swamp, Mangaia, southern Cook Islands.

10

grows best in a true pond-field, were constructed particularly in the Cook, Hawaiian and Society Islands. Elsewhere, it was widely grown as a dry-land crop by rainfall gardening. Another aroid, *Cyrtosperma chamissonis*, was grown in pits excavated to the water-table on certain atolls, but this plant was of more importance in Micronesia than in Polynesia.

A number of other plants of South-East Asian origin were cultivated by the Polynesians; these included the paper mulberry tree (*Broussonetia papyrifera*), which provided an inner bark used for making felted cloth (*tapa*), and the small shrub *Piper methysticum*. This had a root which was chewed and mixed with water to provide a stupefying drink known as *kava*, and the drinking of *kava* was an important aspect of many ceremonies in western Polynesia and Fiji.

11

We come finally to the sweet potato, which is certainly of Andean origin on both linguistic and botanical grounds.[18] It is not known how it reached Polynesia, but the hand of man seems likely; this need not of course imply a massive colonization by South American Indians. The plant was grown in the Hawaiian Islands, Easter Island and New Zealand, and on a very small scale in the Society and Marquesas Islands. Being relatively hardy it was of particular importance in temperate New Zealand and Easter Island, and never really thrived in truly tropical areas. It was possibly introduced into Polynesia, perhaps to the Marquesas, about 1000–1500 years ago, and it is not yet clear whether it ever reached western Polynesia or Melanesia in prehistoric times.

The most widespread system of cultivation in Polynesia was shifting horticulture, wherein a plot was cleared, the vegetation burnt, and plants set in individual holes made with a digging stick. The plot would be planted for perhaps two or three years, and then left to revert to fallow – normally of small trees and thick undergrowth – for perhaps 10 or 15 years. Plots were not tilled and the Polynesians did not use the plough. Their crops were not propagated by seed, but rather by vine cuttings, tuber tops or sprouts. Such vegetative reproduction is common to South-East Asia and the Pacific Islands, and is of course intimately associated with non-cereal plants. It has often been pointed out that this type of shifting horticulture, wherein a number of different species of plants are often planted together in one plot and the plot itself finally left for a long fallow, is well integrated with the natural processes of soil regeneration in the tropics. Obviously, if over-population leads to undue pressure

on the system, then proper regeneration does not take place and virtually uncultivable grasslands may develop, but this never seems to have happened to any appreciable extent in Polynesia. The Polynesians never depended heavily on shifting cultivation, and utilized more stable plantations of trees – such as coconut and breadfruit – on a much larger relative scale than did the peoples of Melanesia and South-East Asia.

The technique of wet-taro cultivation was the main form of horticultural intensification practised in Polynesia, and it is on a par with the wet-rice cultivation systems of South-East Asia. The taro was grown in rectangular plots of varying size, surrounded by banks to hold a few inches of standing water. These plots were often constructed as terraces along the sides of streams, the water being fed in by ditches and allowed to flow from one terrace to another, or they could (as in the case of Mangaia) be constructed in swamps. However built, they needed a gradient to allow the water to move slowly, to avoid stagnation. Irrigated plots of this kind did not need long fallows, and this highly intensive and productive cultivation of taro supported very large populations in many parts of eastern Polynesia. In western Polynesia there is less evidence for its use, since yams were more important in Tonga, and in Samoa it appears that taro was normally grown by shifting cultivation using heavy rainfall. Several large wet-taro terracing systems have been surveyed in

11 A Tongan chief (centre) officiating at a *kava*-drinking ceremony. The *kava* is being mixed in the wooden bowl at rear centre. Drawn by John Webber on Cook's third voyage, 1777.

the Hawaiian and Cook Islands, and in the Hawaiian Islands recent excavations[19] have shown that they date back to the fourteenth century in one valley (see page 106). The Polynesians probably practised this technique from the early days of their settlement in Polynesia, but only with the large, dense populations of later prehistory did it become really important.

The above descriptions of plant cultivation apply mainly to the high tropical islands. On atolls only coconuts and pandanus would normally grow, owing to the absence of soil, although industrious populations could make soil by composting rotting vegetation, and aroids could be grown in pits, as noted above. Easter Island, being outside the tropics, would not support coconut or breadfruit, and New Zealand is a very special case which demands a separate description, since the Maoris were the only Polynesians to adapt to a totally temperate climate.

The two main islands of New Zealand stretch over 12 degrees of latitude, with a range of coastal, volcanic and alpine landscapes not found elsewhere in Polynesia. In the warmer coastal parts of the North Island yam, taro and sweet potato could be cultivated, and the last-named was stored through the winter in roofed underground pits (see page 157). The other tropical crops naturally would not grow at all, and most of the South Island supported only hunters and gatherers, until Europeans introduced the hardy white potato. The sweet potato had to be grown by seasonal shifting cultivation, and although the most important of the introduced plants, it was eclipsed in production by the rhizome of the native fern, *Pteridium esculentum*. New Zealand coastal conditions also led to a much higher dependence on shellfish than elsewhere in Polynesia.

Polynesian fishing methods will be taken up in later chapters, and it only remains here to mention the three domesticated animals; the dog, pig and chicken. These are of South-East Asian origin, and like the plants they had to be carried into Polynesia in the canoes of the first settlers. Many small islands and atolls would apparently not support any domesticated animals at all, and only the dog reached New Zealand, and the chicken Easter Island. However, on the larger islands in Hawaii, the Societies and Samoa, we find all three, together with the ubiquitous rat (which was occasionally eaten too). In general these animals were not eaten with any regularity, and many stocks seem to have been monopolized by chiefs and temple establishments. They were, as in Melanesia, often killed in large numbers for feasts, but as everyday meat supplies they were far eclipsed by fish.

## Polynesian canoes and navigation[20]

To understand the real achievements of the Polynesians one needs to lie on the hard, smelly deck of a wallowing copra ship for a week or so; this is about all the average landlubber without a yacht can do these days, and it is a salutary experience never to be forgotten. The early Polynesians underwent hardships which few modern men could even visualize. The 4000-kilometre voyage from the Society to the Hawaiian Islands may occupy only a few inches on a map, but in a partially open canoe laden with men, women, children, animals and precious seed plants it must surely have been an appalling ordeal. The astounding fact is that the Polynesians reached virtually every island within the huge Polynesian triangle, although by no means all were actually settled.

The basic canoe of the Polynesians, as of most of the Oceanic peoples, was of dug-out type with an attached balancing outrigger which was kept to windward. Such canoes could be sailed or paddled, but being small were mainly restricted to fishing and inshore activities. The Micronesians developed their outrigger canoes into the fastest and most manoeuvrable long-distance voyaging vessels in the Pacific, by the addition of travelling platforms and lateen sails which could be swung from one end to the other to change direction. The Polynesians constructed a different type of canoe for voyaging, which consisted of two large equal-length hulls lashed side by side.

The hulls of these Polynesian double canoes were built up carvel-fashion from planks lashed edge to edge through caulked holes. They were used widely in eastern Polynesia, although the Tongans and Samoans had by European contact adopted a Fijian type with unequal hulls, perhaps related to the Micronesian outriggers. The Maoris of New Zealand had also virtually stopped making double canoes by Cook's time, and produced instead magnificent single-hulled war canoes with high carved sterns. Otherwise, however, double canoes were in quite common use at European contact, and they probably represent the form used on the earliest Polynesian migrations. In Tahiti Captain Cook was able to review a splendid war fleet of an estimated 160 double war canoes, some up to 30 metres long. As did the Maoris, so the Tahitians also carved remarkable stern pieces up to 8 metres high, to judge from Hodges's illustrations. The Tahitians indeed used their fleets for naval warfare, and the warriors leapt from one canoe to another to fight hand to hand on

12

13

14

12 A New Zealand single-hulled war canoe. Drawn by Sydney Parkinson on Cook's first voyage, 1769.

13 A double canoe of Raiatea, Society Islands. Drawn by Sydney Parkinson on Cook's first voyage.

14 A war fleet of double canoes in Tahiti. Drawn by William Hodges on Cook's second voyage, 1774.

raised platforms. These war canoes were of course paddled, but sails were also used commonly, and in Polynesia were in a fixed vertical position, which necessitated tacking to change direction. The Tuamotuans did develop a lateen sail which could be swung around like the Micronesian ones, but this may have been an independent development.

Of course, having a fine double canoe is only half the battle. One still has to sail it without a compass or a sextant, and it is over Polynesian voyaging abilities that some quite vituperative recent arguments among scholars have risen. The problem is that we have no really good account of ancient navigation techniques in Polynesia, although we certainly do for Micronesia, where many prehistoric techniques of navigation are still used. The Polynesians of Cook's day had in fact stopped making exploratory voyages into the unknown, although they were perfectly capable of sailing between known destinations in single or adjacent archipelagos, over distances up to 400 kilometres. The Society and Tuamotu Islanders were doing this, and the Tongans also were making regular trips to Samoa and Fiji. We know from Cook and Andia de Varela, a Spaniard who visited Tahiti in 1774–5, that the Tahitians used the rising or setting positions of stars, as well as wind directions (which can be quite regular in these latitudes at certain seasons). They rarely became lost, and according to Varela reached their destinations 'with as much precision as the most expert navigator of civilised nations could achieve'.[21] The Tahitians also had a broad geographical knowledge of most of the islands in tropical Polynesia, but apparently not of New Zealand, Hawaii or Easter Island.[22] Whether this knowledge represents folk-memory, chance arrivals, or actual Tahitian visits we shall probably never know.

The major problems arise when we come to ask how the Polynesians settled distant islands in unknown waters in the early years of their expansion. In the late nineteenth and early part of this century, most scholars believed that they were capable of voyaging to new islands right across the Pacific, and of finding their ways home afterwards. This is of course what many traditions imply, although the danger here is that these traditions have incorporated geographical knowledge derived from Europeans; Polynesians were travelling around on European ships right from Cook's time. A number of people have always been rather sceptical of the nineteenth-century romantic view, rightly or wrongly, and perhaps the best-known sceptic was the late Andrew Sharp, whose controversial work appeared in final

form in 1963.[23] Sharp's view was that Polynesians had no means of determining longitude and could not measure the displacement caused by currents; hence they might be able to reach distant islands, but would never find their way back home again. This hypothesis of 'one-way voyaging' caused quite a ripple in the Polynesian scholastic pool, although it should be noted that a one-way voyage is not necessarily a drift voyage; Sharp has often been misunderstood on this point.

We know, indeed, that the major Polynesian settlements were not from drift voyages, partly because viable populations of humans, plants and animals got through as well, and it is unlikely that these would be carried on some mere drifting fishing canoe. Furthermore, the computer results mentioned briefly on page 13 have shown that it is virtually impossible to drift to many parts of Polynesia, and intentional sailing into the wind must have taken place. If Polynesia had been settled entirely by drifters, then there would probably be no Polynesians in certain areas such as Hawaii, Easter Island and New Zealand.

15 The *Hokule'a* en route from Tahiti to Hawaii in 1976.

At the present time the debates about Polynesian navigational skills continue. Some agree with Sharp, others say he went too far in a negative direction. Recent records of Micronesian voyaging techniques may be of help, for people here still make long-distance voyages to known destinations without instruments.[24] In 1976 a replica of a Polynesian double canoe (called the *Hokule'a*) was built in Hawaii and sailed from Maui to Tahiti with a Hawaiian crew and a Micronesian navigator. The canoe had no instruments, and the successful trip navigated by star positions and wave patterns over almost 5000 kilometres took 35 days. It carried a crew of 15 men (plus two photographers), together with traditional foods and livestock, and all thankfully survived except for the taro. On arrival in Tahiti the crew were tired and extremely tense, as one would expect from the conditions which they had had to endure. Although no scientific report is yet available,[25] it is clear that the *Hokule'a* will make a dramatic impact on scholastic discussions of Polynesian voyaging ability.

My own view, which is not based on practical experience, is that many distant areas of Polynesia, such as New Zealand and Easter Island, were settled by one-way intentional voyages. However, it may well be that two-way voyaging in tropical Polynesia was much more extensive 1000 years ago than it was in 1769. The great problem is to prove this, and indeed such theories may never be susceptible to acceptable scientific proof. We can only now admire the achievements of the people whom Sir Peter Buck once called 'The Vikings of the Pacific'.

# 3

# The origins of the Polynesians

At the present time, the earliest traceable homeland of the Polynesians can be located somewhere among the later Neolithic cultures of the Philippines and eastern Indonesia, in the period between 1500 and 1000 BC. The subsequent movements of early Polynesians through the region of Melanesia can be traced clearly through the distinctive ceramics of the Lapita Culture (*c.* 1500–500 BC), and these have been found in sites from northern New Guinea right through to Tonga and Samoa. In turn, the Lapita ceramics may be derived from ultimate predecessors in the Philippines, Sulawesi or the Moluccas, as we shall see below. It is rather pointless at present to speculate on the Polynesian ancestry prior to the Neolithic, although the Mongoloid populations which now inhabit Island South-East Asia and Polynesia may well have an origin on the mainland of eastern Asia. This origin is certainly in excess of 6000 years ago, and cannot yet be traced with specific reference to the Polynesians in any meaningful way. Linguistically (as speakers of Austronesian languages), archaeologically and racially the Polynesians are demonstrably of Indonesian-Philippine origin.

The prehistory of South-East Asia is now quite well known through intensive recent work.[1] On the mainland, Neolithic cultures with cord-marked ceramics and ground stone adzes were widely established by 6000 BC, and assemblages of this type also appear in Taiwan after 4000 BC. Unfortunately, we have very little information on this period from Sumatra, Java or Borneo, but the picture is better for the islands to the east. In the Philippines, Sulawesi and Timor a number of sites have been excavated containing plain pottery, without cord-marking but sometimes red-slipped, dating from the third millennium BC. These sites follow earlier pre-ceramic industries with unground flake and blade tools, and it seems to be a reasonable assumption that they signal the spread into the region of horticultural people with pottery, tame pigs, ground adzes of stone and shell, and a developing ability in ocean navigation. Linguistically we can correlate these people with a population of early Austronesians, and they surely represent the origin pool from whom the Polynesians were later to be drawn.

So far, no traces of this early kind of plain pottery have appeared in New Guinea or Melanesia, and this area seems to have been developing along its own lines with little contact to the west. The earliest pottery found so far in Melanesia belongs to the Lapita Culture described below, and this postdates 1500 BC. However, in the New Guinea Highlands people were draining swamps, perhaps for taro cultivation, by at least 4000 BC,[2] and they also had tame pigs by this time; as a non-native to New Guinea the pig was certainly introduced from the Indonesian islands to the west. As discussed on page 24, Melanesian peoples speaking Austronesian languages had probably spread by 3000 BC through the Solomons and New Hebrides to as far as New Caledonia, although most of our information on the earliest Austronesian speakers in the islands of Melanesia to the east of New Guinea comes from linguistics (see page 28), and archaeologically we are very much in the dark. We can say, however, that these people were not closely connected with the ancestry of the Polynesians, and they were in fact the ancestors of the present Melanesian peoples of the region. They were probably horticulturists, but this cannot be demonstrated conclusively. The early Polynesians doubtless settled among them, and traded and intermarried with them during their remarkable thrust eastwards.

Returning now to the Philippines and eastern Indonesia, we pick up the thread of Neolithic development after about 1500 BC, when decorated pottery makes its first appearance in the area. In the Batungan Caves on Masbate Island in the central Philippines, Solheim[3] has excavated a ceramic assemblage containing a small percentage of red-slipped sherds from vessels with horizontal rows of decoration on their upper surfaces. The decoration includes rows of stamped circles, incised scrolls and rectilinear designs, and motifs composed of impressed dots arranged in lines. Some of the incisions also have a white lime infill. This assemblage dates to around 1000–750 BC, and the general format of decoration is very close to the Lapita pottery of Melanesia. The Batungan site is a little too late to represent a precise ancestor for Lapita pottery, but further work in the general area will no doubt fill in the missing links, for pottery rather similar to the Batungan sherds has also been found at a

16

similar date on the islands of Palawan and Timor. Some of these sites have also produced small untanged stone adzes of a widespread South-East Asian type, a type ancestral to the later and more elaborate Polynesian forms.

16 Sherds with stamped decoration from the Batungan Caves, Masbate Island, central Philippines.

Now that the South-East Asian background to Polynesian culture has been partially sketched in, we can turn to the Lapita Culture itself, perhaps the most important archaeological discovery of the last twenty years in the Pacific.

## The Lapita Culture[4]

The Lapita Culture provides an admirable record of the rapid movement of mobile Polynesians, eastwards from New Guinea to as far as Samoa, between 1500 and 1000 BC. Lapita sites in Melanesia are generally found in coastal situations or on small offshore islands, and the people who settled them were almost certainly in contact with the very different and probably much larger Melanesian populations already settled in the region. The Lapita people who settled in Melanesia later became absorbed into these Melanesian populations, and only a few racial and ethnographic traces of them survive today. For instance, peoples who partially resemble Polynesians are still to be found on the south coast of Papua, in parts of the New Hebrides, and in Fiji (see page 51), and cultural traces may survive in pottery manufacture, tattooing motifs, certain forms of hereditary chieftainship, and perhaps some kinds of wood carving. The Lapita voyagers who entered Polynesia had a very different history; they entered a huge island world devoid of men, and founded the societies which we now call Polynesian. The present Polynesians are the direct and, as far as we know, uninfluenced descendants of these intrepid voyagers of 3500 years ago.

The Lapita pottery itself is highly distinctive and, when decorated, is easily distinguished from all other Melanesian ceramics. It is usually sand-tempered, fired in open bonfires, and the most common form is a globular or shouldered cooking pot without decoration. However, the decorated sherds, which represent between one and thirty per cent of total site inventories (decoration is much rarer in later sites) are often red-slipped, and come mainly from open bowls with flat or round bases, sometimes with sharp carinations, sometimes with evenly
17 everted sides. The decoration is on the upper surface of the pot, and arranged in horizontal bands as on the late Neolithic pottery of eastern Indonesia and the Philippines. It was done by incision, or by stamping with a toothed implement probably like the widespread Polynesian tattooing chisel. These tools were probably made of wood in various shapes, and none has survived. However, the resulting 'dentate-stamped' motifs are the hallmark of Lapita pottery wherever it is found.
18 The basic Lapita motifs range from rows of simple parallel lines and curves, to complex anthropomorphic representations. The more elaborate geometric forms include eye-motifs, rope-like and arcade designs, rectangular meanders, interlocking Y's, shield-like designs and stamped circles. These motifs are all paralleled in eastern Indonesia and the Philippines, but the Lapita pottery exhibits a certain magnificence which undoubtedly results from constant and successful decorative innovation. It is

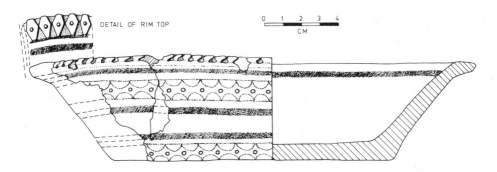

17 Dentate-stamped Lapita bowl from Nenumbo, Gawa, Santa Cruz
Islands, *c*.1000 BC. *Top:* photo of base. *Bottom:* drawn from side view.

49

18 A representation of a human face on a Lapita sherd from Nenumbo, Gawa, Santa Cruz Islands.

unlikely that Lapita pottery *per se* will ever turn up in Island South-East Asia; this area simply provided the people and the basic ceramic knowledge.

One of the remarkable things about Lapita pottery is its widespread homogeneity; identical motifs are found throughout the vast area of settlement from New Britain to Samoa.[5] This area was settled within a time span of perhaps only 300–400 years, and a high degree of contact was clearly maintained for several centuries. In the Melanesian islands the Lapita decoration continues, with some attenuation, down to about 500 BC, and after this time the culture as an entity disappears, leaving only traces to survive to the ethnographic present. In Fiji, Tonga and Samoa the decoration fades more rapidly, and most of the pottery is plain by 500 BC. In the Tongan and Samoan Islands, which belong culturally and geographically in Polynesia, pottery making ceases soon after the time of Christ, and aceramic assemblages follow with no break in continuity to the present. In Fiji the Lapita pottery is replaced after 500 BC by other Melanesian ceramics, although the Fijians, more than any other peoples of Melanesia, have preserved very strong traces of a Lapita ancestry throughout the physical, social and material domains. The present Fijians are in fact a very important population, intermediate in most respects between Polynesians and Melanesians, and this befits their geographical position. Most ethnologists have grouped the Fijians with the Melanesians in the past, however, and the major component of the present population is probably of Melanesian rather than Polynesian origin.

I shall be returning to the subject of the Lapita sites of Tonga and Samoa later; for the moment it is necessary to summarize other known aspects of the Lapita Culture. Marine fishing and shellfishing were certainly major aspects of the economy, and the coconut, pig and fowl are attested archaeologically; the other major Oceanic plant foods, with the exception of the sweet potato, were presumably present too. Although no actual house remains have yet been excavated, it is known that Lapita sites may cover up to 1.5 hectares[6] and earth ovens are commonly reported. Other artefacts include untanged stone adzes with quadrangular, lenticular and plano-convex cross-sections, and these, quite different from the rounded and polished axes made by the Melanesians themselves, are ancestral to Polynesian forms. Shell was also used for adzes, knives, bracelets and necklace units, and there are rare examples of shell fishhooks and bone tattooing chisels.

Obsidian, a sharp volcanic glass used for stone tools, was used widely in the western sites; recent spectrographic analyses have shown that much of it was quarried from the Willaumez Peninsula on northern New Britain, and from there taken as far as New Caledonia,[7] up to 2600 kilometres. Oven stones and cherts were also carried over shorter distances in the southern Solomons, and it is now very clear that the Lapita people were capable of a high degree of sea-going mobility. However, there is no evidence that large quantities of material were being transported, and while it is very likely that they also traded with the surrounding Melanesian populations, this cannot yet be proven. Nevertheless, complex patterns of local trade have always characterized Melanesian society, and the Lapita Culture is hardly likely to be an exception. Regardless of trading capacity, it is quite clear that the Lapita people were efficient colonizers, and their voyaging technology, perhaps with double canoes, was surely ancestral to that of ethnographic Micronesia and Polynesia.

The Lapita Culture therefore provides the necessary archaeological evidence for tracing the Polynesians in a very direct way. By 1300 BC Lapita settlements were made in Tonga, and by 1000 BC in Samoa. Beyond Samoa there is no true Lapita pottery, and the story of the settlement of eastern Polynesia will be told later. However, Lapita transmissions to later Polynesian cultures include the prototype Polynesian adze kit, tattooing chisels and probably fishhooks, as well as other items of lesser significance in the archaeological record. Many features of the Polynesian social system, with its emphasis on aristocratic ranking, were almost certainly present too, although there are few parallels for this remaining now in the ethnographic record of Island South-East Asia.

In terms of physical anthropology, the Lapita evidence ties in geographically with the Mongoloid origins of the Polynesians in Island South-East Asia, but as there are still no large skeletal assemblages from any Lapita site, no direct physical link is available yet from the archaeological record. W. W. Howells[8] has recently suggested that Polynesia was settled via Micronesia, and of course in racial terms the Polynesians are much more closely related to the Micronesians than they are to the Melanesians. Nevertheless, the evidence of the Lapita Culture stands strongly for a settlement via Melanesia, and this is the view I am presenting here. The Micronesians of the Carolinean, Marshallese and Gilbertese atolls may indeed have a Lapita ancestry too, perhaps via the New Hebrides.[9] The apparent absence of Lapita pottery in Micronesia may reflect no more than environmental factors; atoll-dwellers have no clay.

Linguistically, the Polynesian languages are grouped with the Oceanic languages of Melanesia, and at first sight this could appear to be a problem. Most linguists, except for Isidore Dyen,[10] are unwilling to postulate direct links between Polynesian and any Philippine or Indonesian languages, and it could be that the early Polynesians adopted local Melanesian languages during the period of the Lapita Culture. I personally regard this as unlikely, and feel that linguists may be underestimating, or simply not investigating, possible links with Island South-East Asia. The closest relatives of the Polynesian languages do indeed lie in eastern Melanesia, but many of these may have originated with the Lapita people anyway, possibly in Island South-East Asia, with subsequent borrowing from the diverse and still only weakly classified Austronesian languages of western Melanesia.

The Lapita story is not yet finished, and we must turn now in more detail to the Lapita sites of western Polynesia, and to their later offshoots in outlier and eastern Polynesia.

## Western Polynesia and the Polynesian outliers: 1500 BC–AD 1

It now seems fairly certain that the Lapita people were the first to penetrate into western Polynesia (or into any part of the Polynesian triangle), and since there are no indications what-soever that the region received any other major population influx from outside, then we are justified in regarding the present Polynesians as the widespread descendants of the initial Lapita colonizers. The high degree of Polynesian homogeneity in race and culture undoubtedly reflects this rather tight 'bottleneck'.

At present, the evidence from linguistics and archaeology suggests that the Tongan Islands were the first to be settled in Polynesia, although it must be admitted that one cannot rule out entirely the possibility that Samoa was first.[11] If we accept the present evidence at face value, then the hitherto empty Tongan Islands were settled by Lapita colonists from Fiji sometime before 1300 BC. The main island of Tonga is Tongatapu – a large flat island of raised coral in the south of the group – and the settlers here lived around the edge of a large lagoon which cuts into the centre of the island[12] (see figure 29). Their decorated pottery, very similar to that from New Caledonia and Fiji, has been found in shell-middens around this lagoon, and, as in Melanesia, the decoration fades away over the centuries until all the pottery is plain by 500 BC. By around the time of Christ the making of pottery had disappeared altogether; a rather inexplicable circumstance which occurred in all parts of Polynesia where pottery was once made (i.e. Tonga, Samoa, the Marquesas and some of the outliers). One cannot claim a lack of clay for the volcanic islands, and it seems that, for some reason, the early Polynesians stopped boiling their food and relied instead on the underground earth-oven for baking and pressure-steaming.

The non-ceramic artefacts found in the sites on Tongatapu fall solidly within the Lapita range as described above; the adzes are untanged, and with quadrangular, plano-convex and lenticular cross-sections. There is also a range of shell goods including bracelets, necklace units, pendants, chisels, and a one-piece fishhook. Other Lapita sites are known in the more northerly islands of the group, but nowhere in the Tongan Islands is there an archaeological sequence which extends through the first millennium AD. We have information about the Lapita Culture down to the time of Christ, and we have information about the last thousand years which will be described in the next chapter. But for the development of Polynesian culture in the first millennium AD, when most of eastern Polynesia was settled, we must turn to the Samoan Islands, for which we have a fine and detailed sequence.[13]

Until early in 1973, it was thought that the spread of the Lapita Culture ended in Tonga. In that year, a Lapita site dating from about 1000 BC was found submerged beneath a lagoon offshore from Mulifanua on the western end of Upolu Island in Western Samoa. Little is known of the site apart from the pottery, which is decorated rather simply compared with that in the islands to the west, and which may therefore represent the final limit of true Lapita settlement. Samoa, in fact, seems to occupy a key central role in the culture history of Polynesia. Its language is closer than that of Tonga to eastern and outlier Polynesian languages, and archaeologically we can see several important changes here which underlie a number of later cultures, particularly in eastern Polynesia.

The Samoan islands are mountainous and volcanic like many of those in eastern Polynesia, and the two largest, which now comprise the nation of Western Samoa, are Upolu and Savai'i. The latter word is the same as the name of the mythical Hawaiki found widely as a traditional homeland in eastern Polynesia; a circumstance which may not be coincidental. However, most of our archaeological knowledge comes from Upolu, where a good sequence begins at about 500 BC: the earlier Mulifanua site occupies a somewhat isolated chronological position at present.

On Upolu, a number of excavated occupation deposits in coastal and valley situations on the northern side of the island 19 (see figure 29, Vailele and Sasoa'a) have produced plain pottery dating between 500 BC and AD 200, mostly from simple round-bottomed bowls. This pottery seems to be a degenerate survival of the Lapita wares, and its manufacture dies out soon after the time of Christ. The adzes found in these sites are basically like the untanged Lapita forms found to the west, but since Samoa,

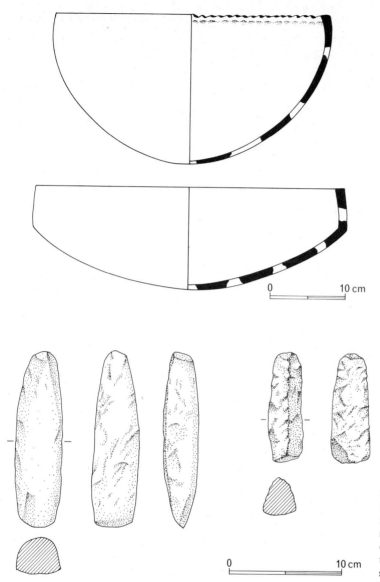

19 *Top:* pottery from Sasoa'a, Upolu, late first millennium BC. *Bottom:* stone adzes of plano-convex (left) and triangular (right) cross-section from Sasoa'a.

like the more easterly islands of Polynesia, has mainly basaltic rocks, a good deal of experimentation in adze production seems to have been carried out. Basalts are more easily flaked than the harder volcanic rocks found in Tonga and Melanesia, and the Samoans developed a new triangular cross-sectioned form of adze never found in Lapita sites, but quite common in eastern Polynesia. Furthermore, the Samoans rapidly discontinued the production of shell bracelets and necklace ornaments, as did the eastern Polynesians, while the Tongans continued to make these articles until European contact. Soon after the demise of pottery, earthen house mounds also appear in Samoa, and these, often of stone or earth, are very common in eastern Polynesia as well. All this suggests that the Samoan Islands provide the best archaeological and linguistic homeland for the first settlers of eastern Polynesia, who probably crossed to the Marquesas or Society Islands before AD 300.

The pattern of settlement in the Polynesian outliers is a little more complicated, and, despite linguistic affiliation with Samoa, it is unlikely that they were settled directly from this group; other western Polynesian groups such as the Ellice Islands or East Futuna (Hoorn Islands) may be more important in this respect.[14] Plain pottery of late Lapita affinity has been found on East Futuna, and also on the outliers of Bellona and Anuta in the Solomons. On Futuna and Bellona the pottery dates to late in the first millennium BC, and it may have been made by early Polynesian settlers on these islands. On Anuta the pottery dates from about 1000 BC, and the excavators think it may be non-Polynesian, with the ancestors of the present Polynesian settlers arriving after AD 500. These islands, geographically part of a long-settled and culturally complex Melanesia, pose many problems which we do not have to face in the Polynesian triangle itself.[15]

The sources of Polynesian culture can thus be traced back to the Lapita Culture of Tonga and Samoa, and further back into Melanesia. We know little of settlement patterns for Tonga, and so far have only relatively unstructured coastal shell-middens. In Samoa, settlement was spreading into interior valleys by 300 BC, and it seems likely that a fully-fledged horticultural economy of Polynesian type had spread over the island of Upolu by this time; this is significant, for all the earlier true Lapita sites are entirely coastal. These early Samoans probably lived in scattered valley and coastal homesteads rather than villages, and they may have stored breadfruit in pits, as did many later Polynesian societies. By AD 400 they were seemingly populous enough to require earthwork forts on some of the higher ridges, and one of these is known from this date above the Luatuanu'u Valley on Upolu. So after the first millennium of settlement in western Polynesia the Lapita Culture had evolved into a more recognizably Polynesian culture, and the greatest feats of navigation ever undertaken by prehistoric men were waiting to be made.

# The great expansion: eastern Polynesia
## AD 300–1200

Between AD 300 and 700 we find the first settlements in the
Marquesas, Society, and Hawaiian Islands, and Easter Island,
and these are associated with an archaeological culture which I
have termed Early Eastern Polynesian.[16] The Cook and Austral
Islands and New Zealand may have been settled during the later
phase of this culture, between 700 and 1100. Basically, this Early
Eastern Polynesian Culture is fairly homogeneous, especially in
its earlier phase, and quite obviously the settlement of eastern
Polynesia began with a very small group of people who again
expanded through a bottleneck, as did the original Lapita people
of western Polynesia.

The bottleneck concept for eastern Polynesia is quite
important, because the Early Eastern Polynesian Culture is
rather different from its contemporary in Samoa. This means

20 Basalt adzes from
Vaitootia, Huahine,
Society Islands. Early
Eastern Polynesian
Culture.

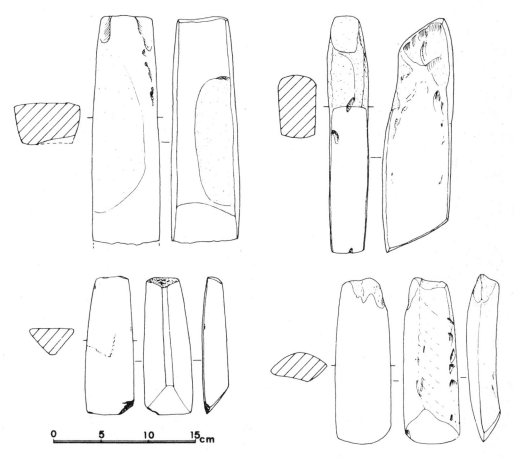

0    5    10    15 cm

that the first settlers of eastern Polynesia made a number of cultural adaptations in the first group to be settled – perhaps the Marquesas or Societies – and took these adaptations with them as they expanded further. The major changes comprise the addition of tangs to stone adzes, and the remarkable development of a range of shell and bone fishing gear, virtually absent in western Polynesia and in Lapita sites.

20

The eastern Polynesian fishhooks of ethnographic times were of three basic types; one-piece bait hooks used for angling, larger two-piece bait hooks with separate points and shanks, and the two-piece trolling hooks used behind a moving canoe for catching voracious surface-swimming fish such as the bonito. The trolling hooks did not take a bait, and often had shanks shaped like small fish. A range of these types is shown in figure 21, together with a specialized hook with a stone weight and a cowrie shell lure, used for catching octopus in reef crevices. The earliest sites in eastern Polynesia have only the one-piece bait hooks and the trolling hooks with pearl-shell shanks, as shown in figures 21e–f, 22 and 23. The two-piece bait hooks of wood and bone (figure 21a, j, k) were developed mainly in Hawaii, Easter Island and New Zealand – all areas where pearl-shell is rare compared to the more tropical islands. One-piece bait hooks of stone were also made on Pitcairn and Easter Island, and the earliest New Zealand sites have trolling hooks with stone rather than shell shanks. Bone harpoons were also used in the Marquesas and Society Islands, New Zealand and Mangareva.

21

22, 23

27

Since it is inconceivable that all the eastern Polynesian islands should have developed tanged adzes and shell fishhooks independently, we must assume that these items were inherited from a single ancestral culture beyond Samoa. According to Sinoto[17] this culture was probably located in the Marquesas Islands, which indeed are the only ones in eastern Polynesia to have produced a few sherds of pottery from the earliest sites about AD 300. Recent temper analyses on this pottery indicate the remarkable possibility that some may have been imported from Fiji,[18] so it could indeed have been brought by the very first settlers, perhaps by Samoans who had been trading with Fiji.

The Early Eastern Polynesian Culture is particularly well known from the Marquesas, especially from rock-shelter and sand-dune deposits around the rugged coasts of these islands. The major site known to date lies in the valley of Hane on Uahuka Island,[19] and there is another in Ha'atuatua Bay on Nuku Hiva. The people who lived here constructed pavements

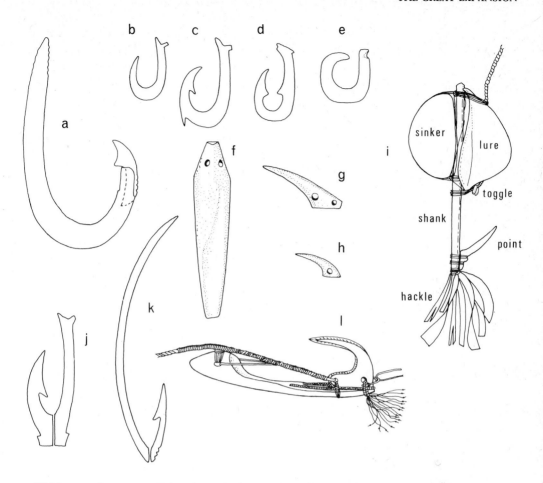

21 Fishing gear from eastern Polynesia: *a–d, j,k* one and two piece bait hook types from Hawaii; *e* early form of Marquesan rotating hook of pearl-shell; *f* pearl-shell bonito-lure shank from Hane, Marquesas; *g–h* pearl-shell bonito-lure points from Hawaii and Borabora; *i* octopus lure of Hawaiian type showing positions of sinker, cowrie shell lure, and point; *l* complete bonito-lure hook of pearl-shell from Pukapuka, showing details of lashings.

for their houses, which were of rectangular shape, and they turned out a fine range of tanged and untanged adzes, shell and bone fishing gear, breast-pendants carved of pearl-shell, and bone or shell tattooing needles and coconut graters. The few sherds of pottery have been mentioned above, and these people also used shaped and perforated whale-teeth and reels of bone for necklace ornaments – these being forms so far absent from the Lapita repertoire, and possibly innovated in eastern Polynesia.

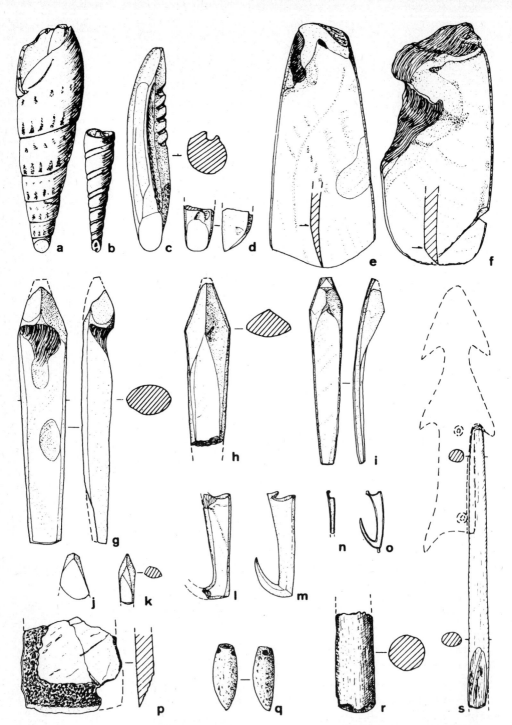

22 Artefacts from Vaitootia, Huahine. Early Eastern Polynesian Culture (37.5% actual size): *a–d* chisels of *Terebra* shell (*a,b*), *Cassis* shell (*c*), and basalt (*d*); *e–f* scraper and coconut grater of pearl-shell; *g–k* pearl-shell bonito-lure shanks; *l–o* pearl-shell bait hooks (*m,n* and *o* from the Marquesas); *p* scraper of turtle bone; *q* shaped pendant of whale-tooth; *r* whalebone object; *s* possible harpoon foreshaft of wood (the harpoon shown in outline is a Marquesan form).

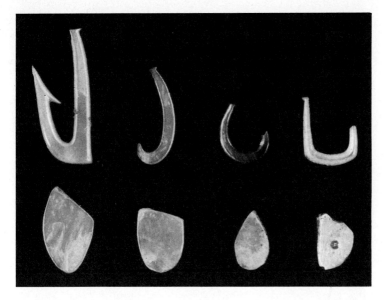

0 _____ 5 cm

23 Fishhooks of pearl-shell and discarded manufacturing tabs from Vaitootia. Bishop Museum, Honolulu.

According to economic analyses,[20] these early Marquesans were exploiting mainly fish, turtles, sea birds and porpoises in the first few centuries, but these activities declined fairly rapidly with time. Towards the end of the first millennium AD horticulture and shellfishing seem to have become much more important, and the introduced pig, dog and rat had become the major meat sources. This pattern of initial exploitation of native resources, followed by quite rapid decline and resulting reliance on horticulture, is found in virtually all parts of Polynesia, and it is seen most clearly in the remarkable prehistory of New Zealand.

Early Eastern Polynesian assemblages of the kind so well known from the Marquesas have also been reported from the Society Islands, especially from a graveyard of extended burials on Maupiti Island, where similar forms of adzes, pendants and fishhooks were apparently laid in the graves with the dead. The Maupiti site dates to between AD 800 and 1200, and Sinoto has recently excavated a slightly earlier habitation site in a waterlogged deposit at Vaitootia on Huahine.[21] The Vaitootia material is quite remarkable, and as well as the usual stone and shell artefacts it has yielded hand-clubs of wood and whalebone of the well-known type produced by the New Zealand Maori of the time of Cook; these are called *patu* in New Zealand, and the Vaitootia evidence is the earliest (*c.* AD 800) we have for this type of artefact in Polynesia. The site has also produced remains of a raised wooden storehouse, a basalt pillar which may have

24

24 Whalebone hand-club of *patu* type from Vaitootia. Bishop Museum, Honolulu.

belonged to an early form of temple, and pieces of sennit cord, coconut shell, pandanus and gourd.

These early Marquesan and Society Island sites are, as is to be expected, similar in content, since both groups were probably settled by the same basic population at about the same time. We know also that the Hawaiian Islands and Easter Island were settled by AD 500–600, but unfortunately no really rich early sites have been discovered in either of these regions, and we know little about the exact origins of their first settlers, apart from the certainty that they were eastern Polynesian. In the Hawaiian Islands, sites at Bellows Beach on Oahu and at the mouth of the Halawa Valley on Molokai[22] have produced adze and fishhook assemblages, but the variety is very restricted when compared with the Marquesas, and this makes comparisons difficult. The Halawa site has also stone kerbs for round-ended houses – a form found in many parts of Polynesia, including Samoa. Both sites also produced flakes of basaltic glass which can now be dated according to the thicknesses of hydration rinds,[23] and these dates provide very valuable confirmation for the carbon-14 results. The Halawa and Bellows sites date from about AD 600–1200.

On Easter Island, carbon dates indicate settlement from AD 500, but few habitation sites of the earliest phase are yet known. The Easter Islanders seem to have been building their famous platforms of stone blocks by AD 700[24] although the statues are later in time. Easter Island will be examined in more detail in Chapter 5, and for the time being I would point out that there is absolutely no evidence, archaeological, linguistic or skeletal, which would indicate an early settlement on the island from South America.

Moving westwards, sites belonging to the later phase of the Early Eastern Polynesian Culture are known from Aitutaki and Rarotonga in the southern Cooks – islands first settled around AD 900 – and we come finally to perhaps the most famous site of all, the burial ground at Wairau Bar in the northern South Island of New Zealand.[25] This site dates to between 1100 and 1350 and its artefacts fit well with the later phase of the Early Eastern Polynesian Culture in the Marquesas and Societies, thus indicating the general area of origin of the first Maoris. Although New Zealand prehistory will be dealt with separately later on, this site is so important that it must be described here. Wairau Bar is a sand-pit across the mouth of the Wairau River, and it was used for burials, the most important being extended burials of men (chiefs?) with moa-egg water bottles, necklaces of bone reels and a range of perforated shark or whale teeth, tattooing needles, harpoons, bone and stone fishhooks, and a huge and magnificent range of tanged and untanged adzes, many apparently unused and perhaps of ceremonial value. Other sites of Wairau type are known from all over New Zealand, but none is as rich in artefacts, and none indicates so clearly the central Polynesian affiliations of the Maoris. The story of economic development in early New Zealand is as fascinating as that of the artefacts, but to this we shall return later.

25-8

The time has come to take stock of our knowledge of early Polynesia. The Lapita settlers quite clearly led a mobile life, possibly under ranked hereditary chiefs, and they expanded with a fully horticultural economy into western Polynesia by at least 1300 BC. Once beyond the already settled portions of Melanesia they could allow their colonizing ambitions full rein, and strong and expansive societies were established in Tonga and Samoa. Links with the area of Lapita settlement to the west, with the exception of Fiji, were soon dropped, since the trade and mobility so important in Melanesia were obviously not so here,

25 Reconstruction of burial 2 (male) at Wairau Bar, with necklaces of bone reels and imitation whale-teeth (left), 14 argillite adzes, and a drilled moa egg.

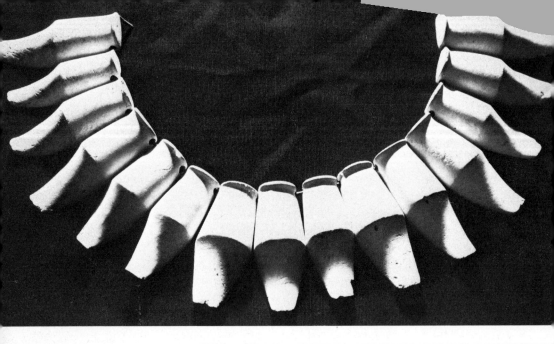

26 (*above*) Necklace of 15 imitation whale-tooth units made from moa bone, from Fortrose, Southland, New Zealand. Presumably of New Zealand Archaic (Early Eastern Polynesian) date.

27 Lure shanks of schist, limestone and serpentine, and a bone point, from Wairau Bar.

28 Finely finished adze of Duff type 1A with lugs on poll, from Wairau Bar, length 47 cm.

and there were no unrelated peoples with whom to trade and perhaps make a profit. The result, especially in Samoa, was a different culture which virtually lacked pottery and which had a new range of artefact types. The eastern Polynesian islands were probably settled initially from Samoa through a bottleneck (the Marquesas?), and the result was a spread of the Early Eastern Polynesian Culture to all remaining groups by 1100. After 1100 the progressive results of isolation and regionalization gave rise to the somewhat different Polynesian cultures which greeted the Europeans of the eighteenth century. By this time some islands had developed very despotic and even splendid chiefdoms, while others had kept to the possibly simpler social forms of an earlier age. The better known of these tropical chiefdoms will now be surveyed.

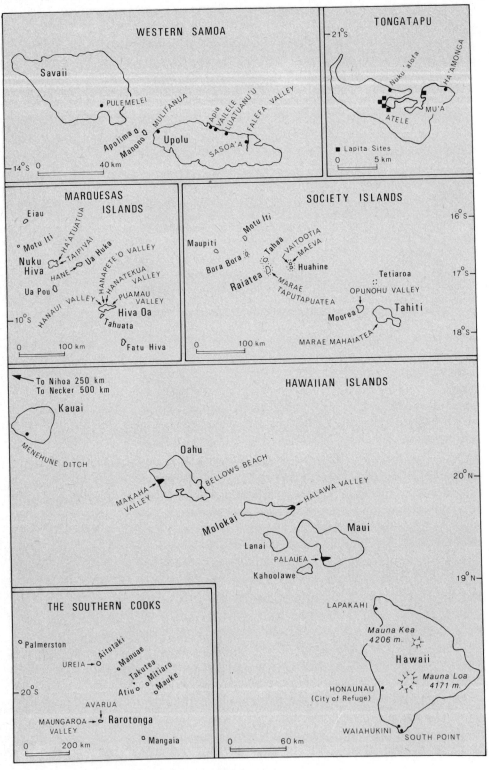

29 Island groups and archaeological sites in Polynesia.

# 4
# The tropical chiefdoms
# (AD 1200–1800)

The societies which developed in tropical Polynesia by AD 1800 each had their own idiosyncrasies, despite the over-all striking degree of homogeneity. In the large populous groups such as Hawaii, Samoa, Tonga and the Societies, highly stratified chiefdoms developed which were capable of a degree of monumental stone construction; the archaeological record in these regions is thus relatively rich. At the other extreme, the inhabitants of the ecologically poor atolls remained basically egalitarian, although the archaeological record on some atolls still has a decided interest. In an intermediate position we have smaller volcanic islands such as the Australs and southern Cooks – these often developed very warlike but generally small-scale societies – and there are also a number of once-settled islands, such as Pitcairn, which had no inhabitants when discovered by Europeans. All these situations make for a fair degree of variety, particularly when we add New Zealand and Easter Island, both of which had such unusual courses of prehistoric development that they will be described in the next chapter separately.

By the time of European contact, the differences between western and eastern societies noted by Burrows (see page 20)

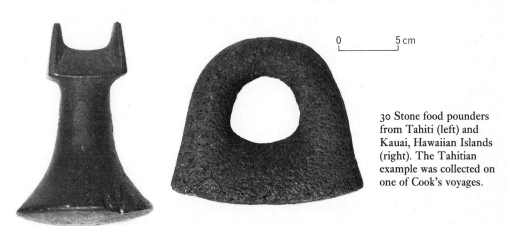

0        5 cm

30 Stone food pounders from Tahiti (left) and Kauai, Hawaiian Islands (right). The Tahitian example was collected on one of Cook's voyages.

were fully formed. Archaeologically, the western societies lacked
30    tanged adzes, stone food pounders, shell fishhooks, and a
number of other items present in the eastern groups. More
importantly, some quite distinct differences in religious
structures had evolved, with the Tongans and Samoans using
timber god-houses for their cults, and the eastern Polynesians
using open-air courtyards with platforms and upright stone
pillars. The eastern structures are generally called *marae* by
archaeologists (the actual word used differs from island to
island), and some will be described later.

Polynesian religion is a topic which any archaeologist would
probably wish to steer clear of, since records of it are often
contradictory and confusing, and different tribes even on the
same island often had slightly differing beliefs. The early
missionaries were of course unwilling to record beliefs which
they regarded as thoroughly misdirected, to the serious
detriment of later scholarship. Nevertheless, we do know that
the Polynesians had a number of gods and heroes who, like those
of the Greeks and Romans, were connected with certain
departmental activities and anecdotal achievements. Among the
heroes the most widely known is Maui, who is said to have pulled
up several Polynesian islands with his fishhook. The four
mainstream gods were Tangaroa, Rongo, Tu and Tane; only the
first-named found in Tonga and Samoa, but all four found
widely in eastern Polynesia. Activities of these gods varied,
Tangaroa usually being connected with the sea, Tu with war,
Rongo with horticulture, and Tane with forests and procreation.
Most populations also created their own special and local gods,
such as the creator god Makemake on Easter Island and the
volcano goddess Pele on Hawaii. The eastern Polynesians also
had legends about the homeland *Hawaiki* – a place not recorded
in the west, presumably because western Polynesia is in fact
Hawaiki itself.

In most islands the gods themselves tended to form a
hierarchy like the human beings who served them, and in the
Society Islands a famous priestly society was formed to serve the
god Oro, son of Tangaroa. Oro in turn seems to have replaced
Tane, originally the major god of the Societies, and this kind of
fluctuation of fortune is as characteristic of gods as of human
dynasties. The details of course differed from one group to
another. While on the subject of religion it should also be noted
that most Polynesian crafts, particularly those requiring high
levels of skill (carving, canoe building, tattooing etc.), were

always practised in combination with religious observances. Since many priests were craft specialists as well it is not surprising that the religious and craft hierarchies were interwoven in intricate fashion.

## The Tongan Islands

After these preliminaries we may now turn to the societies themselves, and we begin in the west with Tonga, which by 1777, when visited by Cook, had developed one of the most highly stratified societies in Polynesia. Cook observed commoners stooping to touch the sole of a chief's foot as he passed, and the Duff missionaries in 1797 observed how a chief simply rode his double canoe over the smaller canoes of commoners in order to reach the English ship. Unfortunately, we have no information for the group during the first millennium AD, but by AD 950 it is possible to use genealogical traditions to reconstruct a history of the ruling families.[1] By AD 1200 the whole group was apparently dominated by the Tui Tonga dynasty which ruled from the district of Mu'a on Tongatapu, and some parts of Samoa were also possibly controlled by Tongans at this time. By about 1500 the dominant political leadership passed to the Tui Ha'a Takalaua dynasty, and in turn to the Tui Kanokupolu dynasty about 1600. Since the late eighteenth century the Tui Kanokupolu line has acquired an increasing political control of Tonga, which it still retains in the person of the present king. The Tui Tonga dynasty retained a degree of ceremonial power until the death of the last Tui Tonga in 1865, and the prerogatives of the title were then assumed by King George I Tupou, the reigning Tui Kanokupolu.

Since no pottery was made in Tonga from about the time of Christ the whole of its later prehistory is aceramic, although occasional pots were evidently imported from Fiji, where the craft has continued right through to the present. A number of surface monuments[2] belong to this period, although all those with traditional or radio-carbon dates fall within the last millennium. These monuments include the famous trilithon 31 called the Ha'amonga-a-Maui in eastern Tongatapu, said to have been constructed about 1200 to symbolize the two sons of the ruling Tui Tonga. The monument is of coral, and the lintel sits in slots in the tops of the uprights. The present king of Tonga has suggested that this monument may also have been used for

recording equinoxes from star positions. It is certainly unique in the Pacific, and remains something of an enigma.

The other monuments of Tonga are mainly mounds of earth, used for burial, for the chiefly sport of pigeon-snaring, or as resting places for chiefs (according to Cook). The large burial mounds of the Tui Tonga dynasty at Mu'a on Tongatapu have fine stepped faces of cut coral slabs, and some are known to cover coral slab burial chambers. The finest of these tombs is called Paepae-o-Telea, and it was possibly built in the sixteenth century; its facing slabs are stepped back at ground level, and some of the corner ones have been cut to an L-shape. Certain examples of this general class of burial mound supported timber houses or shelters on their tops, in which were placed corpses and carved wooden figures. These houses served religious purposes during burial ceremonies, while at other times the gods were invoked in special god-houses constructed in the settlements; these god-houses have not survived archaeologically. Two unfaced earthen burial mounds at 'Atele on Tongatapu have been excavated by Janet Davidson,[3] and each contained an estimated one hundred or more slightly flexed inhumations laid in

32 Chiefly burial mound at Mu'a, Tongatapu, faced with cut coral slabs. Original sketch by James Wilson in 1797.

32

31 (*opposite*) The Ha'amonga-a-Maui, Tongatapu.

33 Round-ended dwelling houses on Tongatapu, drawn by L. de Sainson on the voyage of the *Astrolabe*, under the command of Dumont d'Urville, 1826–9.

33

pits and covered with sand. Some had also been wrapped in black bark-cloth. Presumably these mounds were used for burial of members of local land-holding or descent groups, but so far none of the large burial mounds associated with the ruling families has been excavated, and local feeling would probably prevent such work from being undertaken by archaeologists.

The settlement pattern in Tonga at European contact comprised scattered dwellings, some in fenced gardens with neat gateways, separated by roads and tracks. No definite villages are known, but the major ceremonial centre of the ruling dynasties at Mu'a was obviously quite heavily nucleated, and comprised a ditched and banked enclosure covering about 400 by 500 metres, which contained numerous house platforms for chiefs, their families and retainers, and priests. In the centre was a large open space (the *malae*), and several of the large terraced tombs were situated inside and outside the enclosure. Traditionally, the defended enclosure was built around 1400, and it was extended during the seventeenth century. As far as is known, this is the only example of a prehistoric earthwork fortification in Tonga, although several more were built during the wars of the early nineteenth century.

The Tongans, direct descendants of the original Lapita settlers of Polynesia, therefore emerged into the light of written history as a society governed by a powerful and warlike aristocracy which had in times past extended its influence over a large part of western Polynesia. That aristocracy still survives today, alone in Polynesia, and even in prehistoric times the Tongans came closest to developing a single centralized government for the whole group. Perhaps they never quite succeeded, for the influence of the Tongatapu dynasties was never very strong in the remote northern islands, at least at European contact. It may of course have been much stronger at an earlier date.

## The Samoan Islands

The society which developed in Samoa[4] was rather different from that in Tonga, although both societies emphasized the role of formal councils in decision-making to a much greater extent than the eastern Polynesians. In both areas the council meetings also centred on the protocol of a ritual ceremony of *kava* 11 drinking, and this ceremony was absent in eastern Polynesia. In Tonga, the councils consisted of titled individuals ranked by genealogical criteria in the normal Polynesian fashion, and commoners took no part in the discussions. The Samoans took the unusual step of transferring rank to the titles themselves, and filled them by an elective process which was not restricted purely to the nobles. The Samoan system was more flexible than that of Tonga, and its workings involved a much larger cross-section of society.

At present the Samoans live in large villages, although this pattern is probably post-European, and in prehistoric times settlement was much more scattered.[5] Each modern village consists of a number of relatively autonomous cognatic land-holding groups called *aiga*, and each *aiga* has the right to elect one of its members (usually a man) to a titled position in the council. The holders of such titles then convene periodically in circular council houses for discussions. The titles themselves are ranked, and the ranks are reflected in the seating patterns in the council houses; some titles have only local significance, others confer powers over very large districts, and traditionally even over whole islands. What the Samoans have in fact done is to transfer the emphasis from line of descent to local group in the allocation of political status, although primogeniture and genealogical connections were certainly not neglected entirely, particularly for election to the highest-ranking titles. The whole system was protected by a number of checks and balances, such

34 Perspective sketch of star mound at Vaito'omuli, Savai'i.

as separate councils of title-holders' wives and of unmarried men, and it may be because of the emphasis on achievement rather than birth in political life that the Samoans have survived through the period of colonial exploitation to emerge as one of the proudest, most populous, and most vigorous societies in Polynesia.

As in Tonga, Samoan prehistory since about AD 200 has been aceramic. A large number of surface monuments have been surveyed and excavated; these include terraces or earthen mounds for houses, horticultural terraces, and forts defended by ditches cut across steep ridges. The prehistoric house mounds tend to be scattered in valley and coastal situations; there are no village nucleations. Archaeological evidence indicates that the round-ended form of house, used ethnographically for large dwellings or council meetings, goes back into the ceramic phase, and many abandoned house-mounds still support oval settings of kerbstones. Ethnographic records also indicate that the Samoans maintained open spaces for ceremonies (*malae*), as well as god-houses; the latter were probably built on rectangular or star-shaped mounds. Samoa has what is quite probably the largest surviving prehistoric monument in Polynesia – the huge flat-topped stone mound known as the Pulemelei, on Savai'i. This

34

35

mound covers 60 by 50 metres at the base, and is 12 metres high. At either end there is a slightly sunken ramp to the top, where a few postholes and stone heaps could indicate the former presence of a massive ceremonial house. Many other mounds, walls and roads surround the Pulemelei, which seems to have been the focus of an important ceremonial centre, unfortunately as yet undated.

At present, we have little information about prehistory in the rest of western Polynesia over the past 2000 years, but we can see from the ethnographic record that the region as a whole never attained the degree of homogeneity present in eastern Polynesia. The western Polynesian islands were of course settled for much longer, so their cultures had time to diverge further, and this is seen quite clearly when one compares Tongan and Samoan society. The Burrows concept of western Polynesia is based more on shared retentions from the Lapita Culture than on shared innovations; it is the latter, such as the tanged adzes, fishing gear, stone temples, and a huge range of material, religious and social phenomena, that make the eastern Polynesians into much more of a recognizable unit.

35 Part of one side of the Pulemelei stone mound, Palauli, Savai'i. The figures are standing in one of the sunken ramps.

## The eastern Polynesians

36   Before looking at some eastern Polynesian societies in more detail, we should perhaps examine the main types of temples and stone adzes. In western Polynesia, the rather limited evidence for temples suggests that they were houses constructed either on level ground or on mounds or platforms; very little has survived archaeologically, and the precise uses of these structures are not clear. However, the eastern Polynesians developed large and complex groupings of mounds and courtyards, and most activities took place in the open air, with houses being used mainly for storage of idols or chiefly paraphernalia, and sometimes as priests' dwellings. The eastern Polynesians in general seem to have practised more human sacrifices than their western cousins, and many of these temples (or *marae*), particularly in Tahiti, provided grisly scenarios for the display of offerings.

The earliest *marae*[6] probably consisted of small stone platforms or one or more upright stone pillars. On Easter Island such platforms were built before AD 1000, and a single upright is known from the Vaitootia site on Huahine, dated to about AD 850. Hence these developments away from simple god-houses probably occurred very early in the settlement of eastern Polynesia, and some island groups, such as New Zealand and the northern Marquesas, retained such basic types of *marae* until European contact (although these structures are extremely rare in New Zealand). In the more central groups, such as the Societies, Tuamotus, southern Marquesas, Australs and southern Cooks, the *marae* became rather more elaborate, and often consisted of paved rectangular courts which supported groups of uprights, and a large platform across one end. The term *marae*, with the specific meaning of a stone temple, is also found only in the central groups, and it probably acquired this meaning after AD 1000, when the further regions of Polynesia had already been settled. It is no coincidence that the term for such structures in New Zealand, the northern Marquesas and Easter Island is *ahu*; this is actually the word for a stone platform, and presumably goes back to an early date before the more complex central forms had developed. In this connection it is interesting to note that the Easter Island *ahu* are really of quite simple plan, despite their colossal statues. The Hawaiians used a different term altogether (*heiau*), but this may reflect isolation combined with local linguistic innovation. The factor of isolation

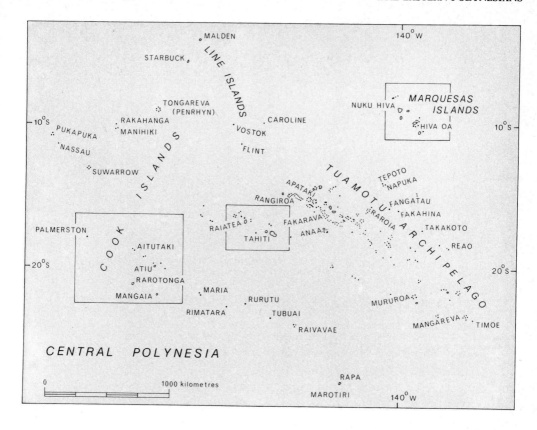

**CENTRAL POLYNESIA**

MALDEN

STARBUCK

LINE ISLANDS

140°W

TONGAREVA
(PENRHYN)

NUKU HIVA

MARQUESAS
ISLANDS

10°S

RAKAHANGA
PUKAPUKA     MANIHIKI

CAROLINE

HIVA OA

10°S

NASSAU

VOSTOK

FLINT

SUWARROW

COOK ISLANDS

APATAKI

TUAMOTU ARCHIPELAGO

TEPOTO
NAPUKA

RANGIROA

FANGATAU

FAKAHINA

PALMERSTON

RAIATEA

FAKARAVA

RAROIA

TAKAKOTO

ANAA

AITUTAKI

TAHITI

REAO

20°S

ATIU
RAROTONGA

20°S

MANGAIA

MARIA

RURUTU

MURUROA

RIMATARA     TUBUAI

MANGAREVA     TIMOE

RAIVAVAE

0          1000 kilometres

RAPA

MAROTIRI

140°W

is in fact very important in any analysis of *marae* architecture, for the degree of variation is actually very large, especially in those islands that were not part of a network of communication; good examples of this are Easter Island and also Aitutaki (page 90).

The eastern Polynesian adzes all begin from a single basic kit, probably developed in Samoa.[7] The earliest assemblages are mostly untanged, like those in western Polynesia, and they have rectangular, triangular or plano-convex cross-sections. By AD 1000 tangs became much more widespread in eastern Polynesia, and after 1300 most groups tended to mass-produce specific types of adzes, thus phasing out the fair degree of variety seen in earlier assemblages.

For instance, the later Hawaiians concentrated on a tanged type with a rectangular cross-section (Duff type 1A),[8] the Maoris produced a similar but untanged form (Duff type 2B), and the central Polynesians (Societies, Cooks, some Australs and Tuamotus) produced a tanged form with a triangular cross-section (Duff type 3A). Most late sites in these groups produce just the one kind of adze signified, and the remarkable variety

36 Map of central Polynesia. For insets see Figure 29.

37

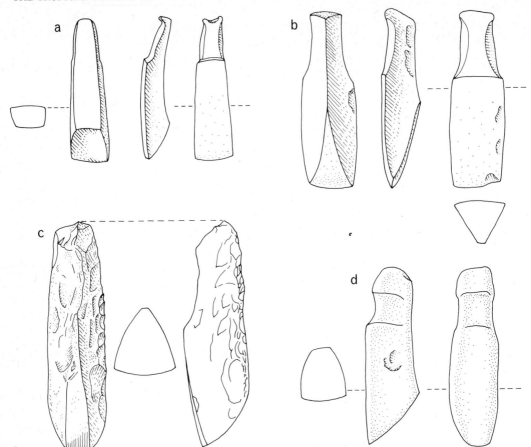

37 Adze types of eastern Polynesia: *a* Duff type IA, Nassau, northern Cook Islands; *b* Duff type 3A, Society Islands; *c* Duff type 4A, Marquesas Islands; *d* Duff type 4D, Easter Island

shown in such early sites as Wairau Bar in New Zealand disappears completely. This circumstance presumably reflects isolation in the peripheral groups coupled with local adaptation; in the central groups there was clearly much more contact, as witnessed by the widespread use of the Duff type 3A. This is a pattern found in all aspects of prehistory; the outer groups diverge, while the central ones (Societies, Cooks, Australs except Rapa, and Tuamotus) retain more homogeneity.[9]

## Tahiti and the Society Islands

In describing the societies of eastern Polynesia, it is clearly preferable to begin with the best-known – the society of Tahiti and the neighbouring Society Islands. The excellent record for this group, recently described in superb detail by Oliver,[10] is certainly better than that for other much-visited groups such as Hawaii, Tonga or New Zealand, and it is incomparably better than those regions left for the rather unsympathetic descriptions of missionaries, such as Samoa and the Cooks. Tahitian society epitomizes the kind of savage magnificence which so attracted the learned gentlemen of the eighteenth century.

The Society Islands comprise two groups: Leeward, including the important islands of Raiatea, Tahaa, Borabora and Huahine, and Windward, including Tahiti itself, and Moorea. These are all high volcanic islands, and at European contact they supported a highly stratified society of perhaps 30,000 people. This society was divided into a number of classes separated by quite rigid barriers against intermarriage; first the chiefs (*ari'i*), then the lesser chiefs and land-holders (*ra'atira*), and finally the commoners (*manahune*). The top chiefly class was further subdivided into two strata, and the bottom of the social ladder was occupied by a rather ill-defined group of slaves and servants, the former generally being war-captives, the latter probably landless *manahune*. The islands of the group at European contact were each divided into a number of independent and somewhat hostile chiefdoms; six are recorded for Tahiti, and one of them (Pare) also controlled the small island of Tetiaroa 40 kilometres to the north. Regular canoe trips were made to Tetiaroa for fish and plantation food.

Tahitian chiefs wielded considerable power over their subjects; they were carried on the backs of retainers, and subjects had to bare the upper parts of their bodies before them. Any commoner's house entered by the chief was afterwards burnt for reasons of *tapu*, and commoners also had to provide periodic tribute in the form of food, bark-cloth, and manufactured objects. Some of this tribute was later channelled back to the common people, but much also went to support the large establishments of relations and administrators living under chiefly patronage. Chiefs also presided over human sacrifices, and were accorded simple mummification after death. Any child born of a chiefly union with a commoner was normally put to death, and infanticide was evidently a standard rule among the Arioi – groups of young men and women who travelled from place to place putting on dramatic and dancing performances. 38

Tahitian society afforded considerable scope for occupational specialization, especially among the various crafts, and certain skilled occupations such as tattooing carried high status. Fishermen were also organized into guilds, and often had their own shrines for worship. The priests who controlled *marae* ceremonies and addressed the gods were normally drawn from

38 Human sacrifice to Oro on a *marae* in Tahiti, drawn by John Webber on Cook's third voyage. An *ahu* with skulls and carved wooden boards (*unu* – to represent gods) is in the background. To the right stand a platform for sacrificed pigs and another larger sacrificial platform covered with bark-cloth.

the upper grades of society, and in earlier times it is possible that the offices of chief and priest were combined in one person. There was also a special class of inspirational priests or shamans – people who affected actual possession by a god during a trance – and men and women from all classes seem to have had access to this occupation. It is unlikely that these specialized activities were actually full-time, for many people, unless they were unusually successful and in demand, probably maintained their own food plantations as well. The Arioi class may also be considered as a specialized one, since its members were fed by the communities they visited, and they could belong to the society for many years, passing through eight grades denoted by tattooed designs. Early accounts of the Arioi indicate a degree of rapacity, cruelty and promiscuity unparalleled in Polynesia; this is especially the case in Tahiti, but we know much less about the cognate institutions reported for the Marquesas, southern Cooks, Tuamotus and Australs.

Traditionally, Raiatea was the island of greatest religious importance in the group, and here, in the district of Opoa, was born the god Oro, son of Ta'aroa (Tangaroa). The great *marae* of Taputapuatea in this district became the centre of Oro-worship, and priests of this god established themselves and their temples in most other islands of the group, including Tahiti. They undoubtedly had much political influence, and they were responsible for the foundation of the Arioi society, traditionally in the sixteenth century. However, although Raiatea was for long the focus of Society Island religion, it is unlikely that it ever wielded secular control over the other islands; indeed, by 1767 it was actually under the control of the chief of neighbouring Borabora.

The *marae* of the Society Islands are the most enduring of the monuments to have survived from prehistoric times. They were first described in detail by Emory in 1933,[11] and normally comprise rectangular courts, sometimes walled, with a platform at one end, and uprights in various positions within the court and on the platform (*ahu*) itself. In the Windward Islands the *ahu* are mainly of coursed basalt or coral blocks, sometimes dressed into shape, while the Leeward Island *ahu* are generally faced with large upright slabs of reef coral. Courts are normally walled in the Windwards, but rarely in the Leewards.

39

40

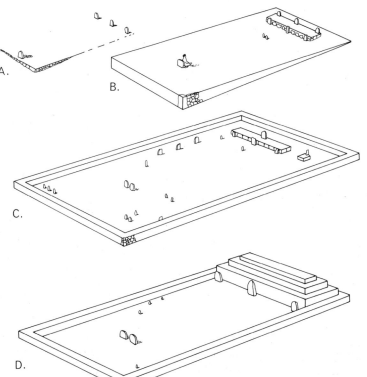

39 Types of Tahitian *marae. a,b* and *c* are of Emory's 'inland' type, *d* is a 'coastal' type. For approximate scale see human figure in *b*.

41     In Tahiti, the largest *marae* ever constructed was called Mahaiatea, built at the behest of the chiefess Purea of Papara district in 1767. This remarkable structure, now destroyed, was visited by Joseph Banks in 1769 and by Duff missionaries in 1797; the *ahu* measured 81 by 22 metres at the base, and rose as a stepped pyramid with 11 steps to a height of between 13.5 and 15.5 metres (the accounts differ slightly). A number of stepped *ahu* of this type do still survive, mainly in coastal regions of Tahiti and Moorea, and surviving records indicate that they were constructed and used by high chiefs; many were possibly dedicated to the god Oro as well. Emory's survey showed that such stepped *ahu* are in a minority, the vast majority of *marae* being much smaller, with small unstepped *ahu* with uprights on top and in front. While the large *marae* may have served tribal functions, and were certainly used for human sacrifice, these smaller ones seem to have belonged to much smaller local groups; the *marae* in fact represented a hierarchy just like the society. Many were undoubtedly used for worshipping local spirits, and some were used by particular specialist groups, such as fishermen. These simple *marae* (called 'inland' *marae* by Emory, as opposed to the larger stepped 'coastal' type) are of a basic plan very widespread in central Polynesia, indicating high antiquity as a class; most of the larger *marae* with stepped *ahu*

40 The *Marae* Taputapu-atea, Opoa, Raiatea, after reconstruction. Bishop Museum, Honolulu.

39

were quite probably built during the eighteenth century. The
dating of these structures is difficult, since they are rarely
associated with stratified occupation deposits, but on comparative grounds the basic court and *ahu* plan had probably evolved
in eastern Polynesia by AD 700.

41 *Marae* Mahaiatea,
Papara, Tahiti. Drawn
from original sketch by
James Wilson, 1797.

The *marae* were used mainly for addressing prayers to gods
and ancestral spirits. Such prayers were necessary for numerous
ceremonies, including declaration of war, investiture and burial
of chiefs, and reception of visitors. The court uprights were used
as backrests for participants and to represent ancestral spirits,
and were sometimes covered with cloth. The *ahu* was sacred to
the gods, who seem to have been represented by carved wooden
boards (*unu*) or stone slabs set on top; it was not mounted by
participants and supported no other structures, and thus served
as an altar. Other structures placed in and around the court
included round-ended priests' houses, raised wooden platforms
for animal sacrifices, pits for the deposition of sacred refuse, and
small portable god-houses for religious objects. Some *marae* also

38

had adjacent paved areas or walled enclosures which held small stone figures (*ti'i*), believed to represent messenger spirits used by the priests for communication with the higher gods; traditionally these figures were not placed in the *marae* proper. Major gods, such as Oro, were represented by wooden staffs wrapped in sennit or by woven cylinders decorated with feathers, and these were kept in storehouses on the main *marae*. 42

The archaeological record in the Societies for the period between 1200 and 1800 comprises large numbers of *marae*, together with low kerbed foundations for round-ended and rectangular houses, horned platforms for the chiefly sport of archery, and an increasing proportion of localized adze and fishhook types indicating some divergence from the widespread norms of the Early Eastern Polynesian Culture. Tahitian society in 1200 was perhaps much less populous and highly stratified than it was six centuries later, and much of the intensification is undoubtedly due to the growth of a large, dense population, as in Tonga, Samoa and Hawaii.

For the over-all settlement pattern in these islands, our best example is the fine survey of the Opunohu Valley of Moorea led by Roger Green;[12] the general pattern is one of non-nucleation, with houses scattered in coastal and valley plantations, clustering locally around large *marae* and chiefly establishments. The Opunohu pattern, representative of the eighteenth century on the eve of European contact, shows that small *marae* and house structures are quite widespread, while the large *marae* with stepped *ahu* and the large round-ended houses are found rarely, and often tend to provide a focus for localized site clusters. There are in fact 56 *marae* in the valley, and Green interprets one as representing the highest status, perhaps the paramount chief, while eight are in a smaller category, and 47 in the smallest household category. Although hard to prove conclusively, it is very likely that this apportionment corresponds to the size and distribution of the major social classes in the valley.

42 Representation of Oro, made of coconut-fibre sennit woven around a wooden core, from Tahiti. Length 50 cm.

## The Tuamotu, Austral and Cook Islands

The Tuamotu Islands form a 1300-kilometre chain of atolls to the east of Tahiti. Those in the north-west were certainly in contact with Tahiti in the late eighteenth century, and were evidently required to supply coconuts, fish, birds, pearl-shell, dogs and mats to the Tahitians. The islands in the south-east were more scattered, and generally uninhabited or only sparsely populated.

However, in the far south-east there lies an important volcanic island (actually several small islands within one lagoon) called Mangareva; this island was thickly populated, had a highly stratified society, and may have been a source for some of the Tuamotuan populations.

Since the Tuamotus are all atolls (except Mangareva), little has survived from prehistoric times apart from the remains of *marae*. We have no archaeological sequence for the group, although it is known that Mangareva was settled by at least AD 1200. The Tuamotuan *marae* are basically like the inland type in Tahiti; they generally have a low *ahu* at one end of a court, and uprights were placed in the courts and on the *ahu*. Some local variation in design is naturally present, and the best examples of this are in the shaped uprights on Takakoto, Fakahina and Fangatau atolls, and in the proliferation of *ahu* uprights found on Reao.[13] The Mangarevan *marae* seem to have been different again; although few have survived, Emory[14] has reported one good example with two steps set into its front, facing on to an unwalled court.

The *marae* in the Tuamotus were apparently put to very similar uses to those in Tahiti; they reflected rank and population distribution, and their appendages, such as uprights, god-houses, storehouses and refuse pits, all fitted the Society Islands functional pattern.[15] Indeed, this basic pattern is common to all the islands of eastern Polynesia with the exceptions of New Zealand and Easter Island.

Unlike the Tuamotus, the southern Cooks and Australs are mostly volcanic islands, and they form a long and scattered line running for about 2500 kilometres in an east–west direction to the south of Tahiti. There is no evidence for prehistoric contact throughout the region, although the three islands of Atiu, Mitiaro and Mauke in the Cooks were in regular contact and under Atiuan domination in late prehistory. Despite the lack of frequent long-distance contact the whole chain, except for isolated Rapa, was occupied by broadly similar cultures related to those of the Society Islands.

The *marae* architecture throughout these islands was quite varied, as a result of the degree of local isolation and adaptation. Raivavae and Tubuai had simple rectangular courts with close-set stone slabs around the edges, up to 4 metres high in the case of one Raivavae *marae*. Raivavae is also well known for its large stone statues, a form of monumental carving shared with Easter Island and the Marquesas, and otherwise not found in Polynesia.

43

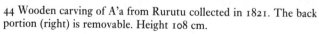

44 Wooden carving of A'a from Rurutu collected in 1821. The back portion (right) is removable. Height 108 cm.

43 (*opposite*) Stone statue from Raivavae, 2.7 m high. Now in the Musée Gauguin, Tahiti.

45 Reconstruction drawing of a Rapan terraced fort, Morongo Uta.

The Cook-Austral chain also produced the finest woodcarving in Polynesia, and one famous piece from Rurutu shows the god A'a  44 (a local Rurutuan divinity) apparently in the act of creating other gods and man. In addition, Raivavae paddles were carved with  47 especially fine surface decoration.

It appears that Rurutu had *marae* similar to those of Tubuai in plan, but for this island we have the added information from Verin's[16] survey of the remarkable village of Vitaria, on the north-western coast of Rurutu. Vitaria consists of at least 60 houses running in roughly parallel lines for about half a kilometre, aligned locally along the parallel streets and around plazas. Villages of this highly nucleated type are very rare in Polynesia, and it is in fact quite hard to explain Vitaria; it was not defended, and may represent nothing more than the results of cultural choice and extreme localization of resources.

The Vitaria houses are all round-ended, and outlined by kerb settings on the tops of rectangular stone-faced earthen terraces. About fourteen *marae* are scattered among the houses, and these generally consist of paved rectangular courts, with or without *ahu*, and surrounded by spaced uprights of basalt. Many of the houses also had lines of backrests set in front of them. The extant Vitaria village clearly belongs to the final phase of prehistory,

46 (*opposite*) Head fragment of staff-god from Rarotonga, possibly representing Tangaroa surmounting successive generations of ancestors. Probably collected in the 1820's. Length 75 cm.

and may even postdate 1800, although the site itself was certainly in use by 1100. It is not known whether earlier settlements on the island were of similar village type.

The other island in the Australs to have received archaeological attention is Rapa, which being rather south of the tropics could not grow coconuts or breadfruit, and which also lacked pigs, dogs and chickens. The Rapan adzes are different from those found in the rest of the Australs, and were clearly developed locally. The Rapans also excavated splendid fortresses on high ridge-junctions, similar in basic concept to the forts of New Zealand. It is interesting that these two southerly islands should have developed fortifications so assiduously, since they are virtually absent everywhere else in Polynesia, apart from occasional examples in Samoa and the Marquesas.

The Rapan forts[17] take the form of central sculpted towers at the junctions of the knife-like ridges on the island, and these are surrounded by lower terrace arrangements in rings or radial lines. Sometimes the terrace scarps were faced with dry-stone masonry. The central towers appear to have been used as citadels and command posts, while the terraces themselves supported houses, sometimes with small shrines set into the earth walls at their backs. The large fort of Morongo Uta was cleared and partially excavated by the Norwegian expedition in 1956; a reconstruction from their report is shown in figure 45.

The Cook islands actually comprise two groups of islands. The northern Cooks are all atolls, basically eastern Polynesian in culture apart from Pukapuka, which on linguistic grounds would seem to have been settled from Samoa. These northern islands have few archaeological remains, although Penrhyn has many *marae* similar to those of the Tuamotus. The southern Cooks are rather more important, and these are nearly all volcanic islands, the largest being Rarotonga, Aitutaki and Mangaia. These islands have long been of importance for studies on ethnology and traditions in Polynesia, and Rarotonga in particular has a splendid tradition of wood-carving. They have also been quite extensively examined from an archaeological viewpoint.[18] At European contact they showed no real unity of culture, since they are separated from each other by quite large distances, and it is rather hard to generalize about them in the sense that one can generalize about the more homogeneous Society Islands. The southern Cooks supported a number of independent chiefdoms – generally several on each island – and traditional history is replete with accounts of local warfare. This was particularly the

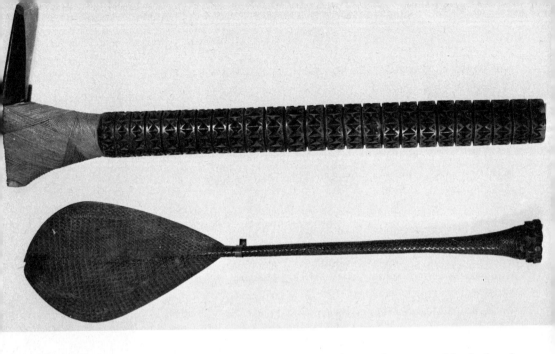

47 *Top:* Mangaian hafted adze of Duff type 3A, with coconut-fibre sennit lashing and carved handle, probably representing rows of stylized human figures. Length 80 cm. Nineteenth century. *Bottom:* carved canoe paddle from Raivavae, Austral Islands. Length 76 cm. Nineteenth century.

case on Mangaia, where political control was vested in the hands of a succession of warrior chiefs, who distributed lands among their followers until they in turn were deposed. Rarotonga had three main tribal areas and four titled paramount chiefs, and was politically more stable than Mangaia despite prolonged periods of fighting. Since populations in these islands were never as large as in Tahiti there are no accounts of such a degree of chiefly power; this is of course to be expected.

Traditions and archaeology suggest that the southern Cooks were settled late in the first millennium AD, perhaps from the Societies, with a possibility of a secondary settlement from Samoa to Rarotonga. My own excavations at Ureia on Aitutaki and at Avarua on Rarotonga have produced restricted assemblages dating from the later phase of the Early Eastern Polynesian Culture, between 950 and 1250, but it is almost impossible to decide on the direction of first settlement; a problem which is present for all eastern Polynesian islands, and which is very much a result of the homogeneity of the early assemblages.

The *marae* architecture of the southern Cooks varies from island to island. On Rarotonga, structures with rectangular courts and *ahu* approximate to the general Tahitian fashion, although *ahu* are here often absent, and the courts themselves may be terraced into a series of steps on sloping ground. Uprights are also rather rare on Rarotonga, and there is a very marked difference here with the *marae* of Aitutaki, which were

entirely without demarcated courts and *ahu*, and comprised one
or more lines of large uprights. The *marae* of Paengariki on
Aitutaki[19] consisted of over 60 uprights about two metres in
height arranged in six parallel rows; the total area covered being
a rectangle of 80 by 40 metres. Although now in ruins, this
structure must once have been a very impressive sight. Finally,
the Mangaian *marae*, and those of Atiu, consisted of simple
earthen terraces faced with shaped slabs of reef coral, sometimes
with rows of uprights on their tops. Some of the Mangaian
monuments are closely paralleled in Rurutu, and some
prehistoric contact is possible.[20]

The patterns of settlement in the southern Cooks are quite
well recorded, and Rarotonga is perhaps the most interesting
island in this respect. This island has a central mountain mass
divided by radial valleys, and surrounded by a flat and fertile
coastal plain up to one kilometre wide. Most of the settlement
was on this coastal plain, but concentrated along a road, called
the Ara Metua, which ran right around the island linking the
tribal districts, and which was paved in some sectors. The road
runs around the inland edge of the coastal strip rather than along
the coast itself, and this position was certainly chosen
purposefully; the Rarotongan coast is subject to occasional
hurricanes, and since the inhabitants utilized the mountain and

48

48 A Mangaian *marae*,
with coral-slab faced
earthen terrace and
uprights.

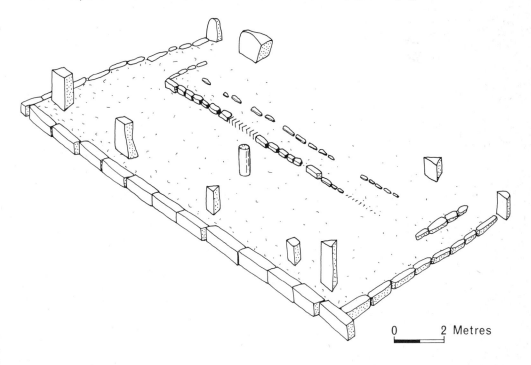

0     2 Metres

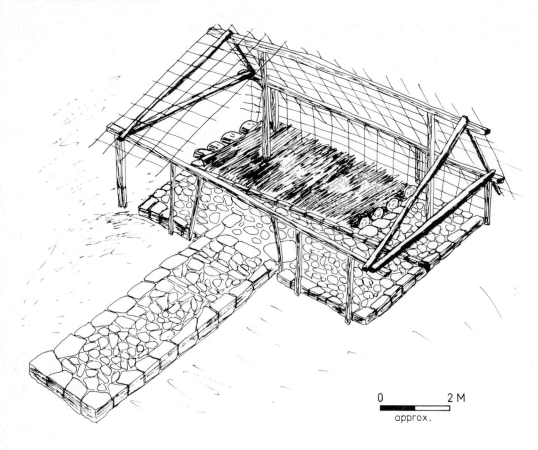

0        2 M

approx.

49 Reconstruction drawing of excavated T-shaped house *paepae* in the Lower Maungaroa Valley, Rarotonga. Late eighteenth century.

valley regions quite commonly, they located their houses and their road in such a position that access time to all resources, including the sea, would be reduced to a rough minimum.

Normally, the Rarotongan valleys were not settled densely, except for the Maungaroa Valley, on the western side of the island, where the members of one tribe occasionally retired to escape the depredations of their warlike neighbours. This remote valley still contains many finely paved house platforms and *marae*,[21] and provides, with the Opunohu Valley and Vitaria, one of the best-preserved community patterns in Polynesia. The Maungaroa dwellings are quite nucleated owing to the scarcity of good level land, much of which was doubtless needed for cultivation, and the larger ones sat on paved platforms across the ends of long paved approach paths (T-shaped *paepae*). As in the Opunohu Valley, it is possible to separate the houses and *marae* into classes according to size and complexity, and thus to reconstruct the presence of a ranked tribal group of possibly 200 persons.[22] Most of the structures belong to the period

49

immediately before 1823, when mission contact was established, but some may date back to 1300.

## The Marquesas Islands

The Marquesas Islands form an isolated but internally close-set group to the north-east of the Tuamotus. They lack coral reefs and have very rugged coastlines and mountainous interiors; the populations lived in deep, narrow valleys which could only be approached by sea or across high ridges, and the resulting political pattern comprised a large number of warlike and virtually independent valley tribes. Social stratification was not as highly developed as in the Societies, although human sacrifice was common, and, like the Maoris, the Marquesans practised cannibalism. They also defended themselves in mountain fortresses defended by steep ditches or stone walls.

Owing to the many rock-shelters found in the Marquesas, it is possible to trace changes in artefact styles from excavated assemblages over time in some detail.[23] New adze, fishhook and ornament types become dominant after 1200, and the dog, introduced by early settlers, rather strangely becomes extinct. However, it is the stone monuments of this group which have always evoked admiration, and a number of detailed surveys have been carried out.[24] Naturally, most of the structures belong to the end of the prehistoric period, since older ones were constantly being rebuilt or demolished, as in any pattern of settlement.

The Marquesans constructed the finest house platforms in Polynesia. The larger houses were placed on high platforms, up to 30 metres long, constructed of finely fitted but unshaped blocks of basalt. These platforms were paved on their tops, and

3

50

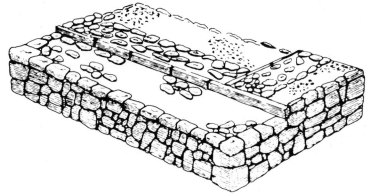

50 A Marquesan house platform, with rear sleeping section slightly raised. Approximately 10 m long.

93

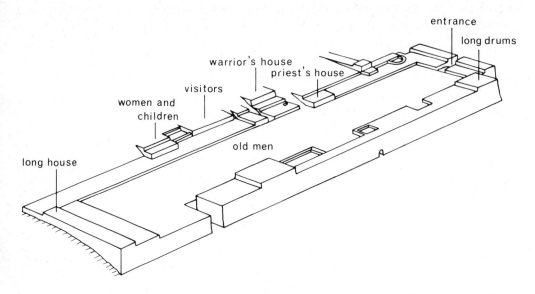

entrance

long drums

warrior's house

priest's house

visitors

women and
children

old men

long house

51 A Marquesan *tohua*.

were often separated by a line of nicely cut slabs of red tuff into an upper sleeping and a lower working area. The rear sleeping area was enclosed on all sides, while the front portion was generally open like a verandah; this basic bipartite house plan is found widely in eastern Polynesia, especially in the Hawaiian and Cook Islands.

The *marae* of the Marquesas generally take the form of quite complex terraced arrangements in the south of the group, while those in the north, especially on Nuku Hiva, would appear to have consisted of god-houses on stone platforms, very like those reported for Samoa. That the northern Marquesas should have retained a form of temple more akin to the western type than anywhere else in eastern Polynesia is probably not coincidental, since these islands may well have been the first to be settled in eastern Polynesia, and it is interesting to note furthermore that the term *ahu* was also retained in the northern Marquesas, as opposed to the more recent term *me'ae* (*marae*) used in the southern islands.

These Marquesan temples were normally built close to inhabited areas, especially to chiefly establishments, although special mortuary *me'ae* were sometimes constructed in secluded areas; these frequently had stone-lined pits set into them for the placing of bones. The *me'ae* of the more public kind were frequently built into much larger ceremonial dancing grounds called *tohua*. The *tohua* are among the most magnificent stone structures on record from Polynesia, and they consisted of a

51

rectangular flat earthen space surrounded by raised stone platforms at various levels. Some of these platforms served as temples, others as seating platforms for various sections of society, and ceremonies accompanied by dancing took place in the court. The *tohua* were used for a large number of ceremonies, including those for the rites of passage of members of chiefly families, and for harvest, memorial and tattooing ceremonies. The largest of the Marquesan *tohua*, named Vahangeku'a in the Taipivai Valley on Nuku Hiva, covered 170 by 25 metres, and was constructed on an artificial terrace faced by a three-metre-high wall of huge blocks of basalt. The excavator of this site, Robert Suggs, has estimated that 9000 cubic metres of soil were moved in its construction.[25]

Other notable examples of Marquesan stonework are the anthropomorphic stone statues found in Taipivai Valley on Nuku Hiva and in Puamau Valley on Hiva Oa. These are generally of red tuff, up to 2.5 metres high, and have the squat, bent-kneed and goggle-eyed posture typically found on wooden carvings throughout eastern Polynesia. Despite Heyerdahl's claim[26] that they represent contact with the famous site of San Agustín in southern Colombia, these statues are of clearly

52

53

52 Terrace facing of *tohua* Vahangeku'a, Taipivai, Nuku Hiva. Courtesy, American Museum of Natural History.

Polynesian type and are found on stone temple platforms, while those of San Augustín are associated with megalithic burial chambers under earthen mounds, a type of monument never found in eastern Polynesia. The general question of American contact with Polynesia will be set before the reader in the next chapter.

Marquesan valleys generally have a high density of house and temple structures along their floors, together with cultivation terraces and walled enclosures. No village planning is evident, and structures tend to be evenly spaced 20 to 30 metres apart. Today these valleys are mostly devoid of human populations, and any person fortunate enough to visit the Marquesas will be undoubtedly moved to wonder at the sight of so much stonework in such a wild and empty setting. The Marquesans, together with their close cousins the Maoris, were by all accounts the hardiest and most robust of the Polynesians, and life was never pervaded with the indolence associated with an island such as Tahiti. Heavily dependent upon the breadfruit – a tree which fruits seasonally and not all year round – they were subjected to famines of devastating proportions, and these naturally increased the incidence of warfare. Many early visitors reported that impoverished and defeated Marquesan families would set off in canoes to find land over the horizon; the majority certainly perished, but we do know that one canoe reached Kaukura in the Tuamotus, where all were killed by the local inhabitants, except for one woman.[27] According to traditional accounts, however, this was not a common fate, and more hospitable receptions were usually accorded to new arrivals on the more fertile volcanic islands.

## The Hawaiian Islands

By comparison with the Marquesas, the Hawaiian Islands, like the Societies, symbolize the heights of Polynesian aristocracy in a setting of ecological lushness. At European contact there were seven inhabited islands in the south-east of the chain, the six major ones being Hawaii, Maui, Molokai, Lanai, Oahu and Kauai. These islands had the highest population of any Polynesian group – possibly 200,000[28] – and, although lacking barrier reefs and lagoons, they did provide large areas suitable for valley and coastal settlement. Hawaii itself is an exception, since much is covered with lava flows from the active volcanoes (the only ones in Polynesia outside Tonga and New Zealand),

53 (*opposite*) A Marquesan stone statue in the Taipivai Valley, Nuku Hiva. Courtesy, American Museum of Natural History.

but even these can erode rapidly to produce soil suitable for cultivation.

As in Tahiti, Hawaiian society was composed of three main strata; high chiefs (*ali'i*), then the lesser chiefs, priests and skilled craftsmen, and finally the commoners. A group of slaves and outcasts may also be regarded as a possible fourth category. At contact the islands were divided into four major chiefdoms, but, as in Tahiti, centralized rule was not achieved until after European contact and stimulus. In 1810 Kamehameha I became king of all Hawaii, as did Pomare II in Tahiti and Moorea in 1815.

The *ali'i* class in Hawaii appears to have severed completely its genealogical links with the commoners, and by the eighteenth century it formed a relatively endogamous group who even resorted to brother–sister marriage to preserve pedigree. The commoners themselves lived in local groups on their land, and chiefs could dispossess people and redistribute land if tribute and corvée labour were not forthcoming, or after success in war. Local stewards called *konohiki* were placed in charge of land divisions; these men were often relatives of the chiefly families. Hawaiian society was therefore well on the way to replacing a system based on traditional kinship with a more state-like form of political organization, and this development was certainly aided by the presence of a very high population density, despite the absence of urbanization. The Hawaiians went further than the other eastern Polynesians towards the achievement of centralized government (only Tonga otherwise competes), and it is no surprise that their chiefs commanded the most sumptuous personal attire recorded in the Pacific; magnificent crested helmets and cloaks set with thousands of red and yellow feathers. Only the gods received similar attention, as we know from the few images of wicker-work and feathers which survived the burning of idols in 1819, and which now grace several of the world's major museums.

On page 62 it was noted that the Hawaiian Islands may have been settled, possibly from the Marquesas, about AD 500–600. There is traditional and some archaeological evidence to suggest later influence from the Society Islands, but this is at present disputed.[29] Nevertheless, it is very likely that the population by AD 1000 was quite large, and Goldman[30] dates the development of the stratified society of late prehistory to between 1100 and 1450. There is also some evidence for an intensification in the cultivation of wet taro at this time, as we shall see, and this of

54 The Alekoko fish-pond
(to right of man-made
wall) at Nawiliwili, Kauai.

course provided the necessary economic basis for the later
developments.

The majority of Hawaiian stone monuments are not quite as
well built as those in Tahiti, Easter Island or the Marquesas,
although this may reflect the rather scoriaceous nature of the
available rock in many areas. There is one irrigation channel on
Kauai (the Menehune Ditch) which has been banked along one
side with finely cut small blocks of stone, but this is the only
structure of its kind in the islands; all other monuments are of
unworked stone. The range of monuments is very large; as well
as the usual house terraces and temples (*heiau*), the Hawaiians
constructed large acreages of field boundary walls, stone
trackways, and stone-walled fish storage areas up to 200 hectares   54
in size in shallow estuaries and coastal lagoons.[31] The latter had
specially constructed wooden grilles to let small fry pass in and
out, while larger fish could be kept inside until needed.

The Hawaiian *heiau* of the major inhabited islands are
generally rather complicated structures, having walls, terraces
and platforms in a variety of arrangements. Much simpler types
closer to the inland Tahitian type were found on isolated Necker   55
Island in 1923;[32] this island, 500 kilometres west of Kauai, was
uninhabited when discovered by Europeans, and it is only one
kilometre long with no surface water. Yet it is dotted with the
remains of no fewer than 33 *heiau* of similar plan, comprising an

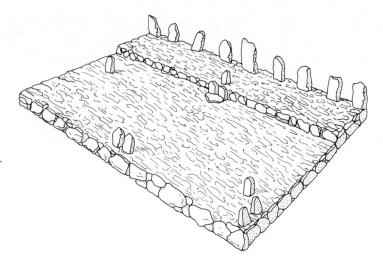

55 A terraced *heiau* with uprights on Necker Island.

56 upper terrace with a line of rear uprights, and further uprights on a lower terrace. One of these *heiau* yielded several male carvings which have free-arm postures similar to those of later Hawaiian wood-carvings. It may be that a group of drifters was once wrecked on the island, and their descendants may have constructed successive *heiau* to the same plan before dying out, totally forgotten in the corpus of Hawaiian traditions. On the other hand it is possible that the island was visited periodically

56 Two stone statues collected on Necker Island in 1894. Heights (left) 48 cm, (right) 29 cm.

for some reason connected with religious activities, but we may never obtain a certain answer. Another little island called Nihoa, half-way between Necker and Kauai, also has numerous *heiau*, and again this island was uninhabited at European discovery. Despite the mystery, these islands are useful in preserving a fossilized form of Hawaiian architecture perhaps several centuries old; hence the stronger relationships with central Polynesia than are found in the constantly reconstructed and modified *heiau* of the major islands.

The *heiau* of the major islands were of course observed in use by Cook and his successors. From the hand of John Webber we have an excellent drawing of a *heiau* at Waimea on Kauai as seen in 1778; we can see the walled enclosure with its rear platform set with wicker-work bundles (probably representing gods), carved wooden slab images,[33] and an oracle tower once covered with bark-cloth and entered by the priests for divine communication. The court has other slab images, a raised platform for sacrifices, a high crested post image, and a stone upright. A house for wooden images occupies the left foreground. This *heiau* in fact poses a number of problems; the site has never been located archaeologically, and in plan it clearly resembles the *marae* of Tahiti and the structures of Necker Island. Stone uprights, for instance, are rarely found elsewhere in Hawaii, and Kauai in its

57

57 The *heiau* at Waimea, Kauai, drawn by John Webber on Cook's third voyage.

westward semi-isolation may have preserved an earlier style of construction; there are other walled *heiau* with uprights on the island, particularly in the Wailua Valley.

Elsewhere in the Hawaiian Islands structures with internal terraces at different levels are more common. This is the case with the recently reconstructed *heiau* Kaneaki in the Makaha Valley on Oahu, where visitors can now see the reconstructed sacred house, drum house, offering platform, idols and oracle towers. The *heiau* of Pu'u-o-Mahuka, also on Oahu, is one of the largest in the group; this has two adjoined walled courts covering an area of 160 by 52 metres, with terraces inside, and an attached shrine. On Molokai the *heiau* of 'Ili'iliopae comprised a huge stone platform 87 metres long, 26 metres wide and up to 7 metres high, with three terraces extending down from its eastern end. Not all *heiau*, of course, attained such a large size, and there are many hundreds of structures varying in size right down to the tiny platforms of fishermen's shrines.

On the west coast of Hawaii at Honaunau (just south of Kealakekua Bay where Cook was killed in 1778) lies the City of

58 The reconstructed *heiau* Kaneaki in the Makaha Valley on Oahu.

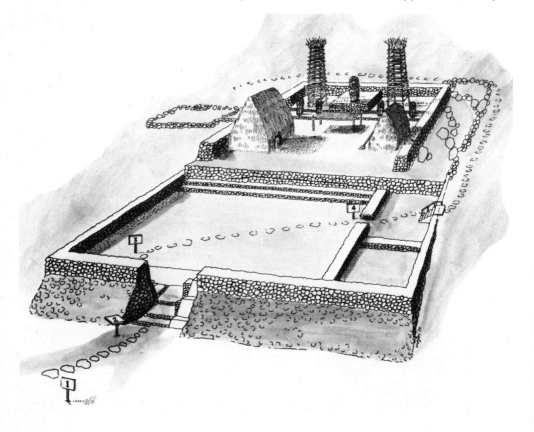

59 The three terraces at
the eastern end of *heiau*
'Ili'iliopae on Molokai.

Refuge, or Pu'uhonua.[34] This structure, which is really without
parallel in Polynesia, comprised a walled enclosure on the end of
a peninsula to which criminals and those defeated in war could
flee for priestly protection. After a period of confinement they
were then allowed to go free without molestation. There are
traditions of the existence of similar places in other parts of
Polynesia, but no archaeological survivals of this complexity.
Within the massive four-metre-high walls were three *heiau*; one
now impossibly ruined, another rebuilt recently to its original
plan (a platform 40 by 20 metres by 2.4 metres high), and a third,
the Hale-o-keawe, now reconstructed in entirety for the
appreciative eyes of visitors. This structure was visited in 1823
by the Rev. William Ellis; owing to its sacredness it had survived
the overthrow of the pagan religion in 1819. It comprised a
thatched house in a paved and fenced enclosure, containing the
bones of revered chiefs tied in bundles, together with numerous
chiefly garments, feather capes, and wooden carved figures.
Large wooden images were set up both inside and outside the
fence, and some from this *heiau* still exist in museums, although
the ones presently on the site are of course replicas.

One of the main developments in Hawaiian archaeology in
recent years has been the increased emphasis on survey and
excavation in discrete valleys; such valley units with adjacent

60 The reconstructed enclosure wall of the City of Refuge, Honaunau, Kona, Hawaii.

61 The Hale-o-keawe at Honaunau, reconstructed as part of the City of Refuge National Park by the National Park Service, U.S. Department of the Interior.

62 Hawaiian wooden
image of the war-god
Kukailimoku. Early
nineteenth century.
Height 2.1 m.

coasts were the main elements of ancient Hawaiian tenure, and were termed *ahupua'a*. This recent archaeological work has told us a great deal about settlement distribution, and the dates and natures of the supporting horticultural systems, and it is this kind of information which allows testable hypotheses about the growth of eighteenth-century Hawaiian culture.

The two major valley projects carried out so far have been in the Makaha Valley on Oahu,[35] and in the Halawa Valley on Molokai.[36] The Makaha Valley is about 7 kilometres long, and being on the drier side of Oahu it has quite a low rainfall in its lower portion. This circumstance had a direct impact on the economy of the inhabitants, for only the upper and wetter part of the valley was used for wet-taro cultivation, in stone-faced terraces fed by culverts from the stream, or by ingenious channels cut back into the hillside to tap the water-table. The lower and middle parts of the valley were used for seasonal cultivation, perhaps of sweet potato, in dry-land fields surrounded by piled rock boundaries. Stone foundations for shelters are scattered throughout the valley, and there are a smaller number of permanent house platforms and *heiau*. However, most of the permanent settlement was probably on the coast – an area now under a modern township. The fields in the lower valley were in use by AD 1100, and the upper wet-taro terraces date from at least 1400, dates which tie in well with those from the Halawa Valley.

58

The Halawa Valley is on the eastern end of Molokai, and much wetter than Makaha. The Early Eastern Polynesian settlement at the mouth of this valley was mentioned on page 62; however, permanent settlement within the valley is not in evidence before about 1250. Small staircase terraces for taro, a little like those in the upper Makaha Valley, were constructed from this time, but there is a more explosive burst of activity after 1500–1600, when much of the lower Halawa Valley was converted into wet-taro beds fed from the stream. The greater part of the valley floor was finally converted to taro cultivation, and fine terrace walls a metre or more in height still survive in very large numbers.

The evidence so far suggests that intensive valley irrigation in the Hawaiian Islands dates only within the past 700 years or so. The earlier sites that have been identified are all coastal, and seem to indicate an economy based on fishing, perhaps with localized irrigation and rainfall horticulture on a small scale. This is in fact the pattern throughout eastern Polynesia, and

63 Parallel field boundaries running along contours at Lapakahi, Kohala, Hawaii.

major inland settlement in islands such as Rarotonga, Tahiti and Moorea seems to be of similar recent date. To use a rather crude metaphor, it is apparent that the populations of eastern Polynesia were generating demographic steam after 1200; hence the blossoming of social stratification and strong chiefdoms in the larger islands.

On Hawaii, the largest tropical Polynesian island (being over 10,000 square kilometres in area), early cultivators had to cope with a very wet (or windward) eastern side, and a very dry (or leeward) western side. The windward side had some wet-taro cultivation in valley bottoms, the most famous now being the Waipio Valley, while the drier leeward side actually seems to have supported a larger population, who used many square kilometres of dry-land rectangular fields surrounded by rock and earth boundaries. These fields are particularly striking in Kohala and Kona, and here cover some 200 square kilometres; the boundaries served primarily as dumps for the many rocks removed from the young volcanic soils, and any extras were simply piled in large rounded heaps. At Lapakahi,[37] a large

63 belt of fields of this type was in use from about 1400, and ethnohistorical accounts indicate the cultivation of sweet potato and some dry taro, together with breadfruit, sugar cane, and bananas in sheltered spots. Most of these fields are found on higher inland slopes where rainfall was sufficient for cultivation, and the people themselves lived in coastal hamlets, separated from the fields by a very dry coastal belt about 2 kilometres wide which was mostly unutilized. This circumstance is illustrated in figure 63.

64 Hawaiian archaeology is not, however, restricted to fields and stone monuments. These islands have the best complexes of petroglyphs surviving anywhere in Polynesia, particularly on Hawaii itself, at Anaeho'omalu and Puako on the west coast, and at Pu'uloa in the south-east. Petroglyphs are virtually impossible to date, except for those showing European influence, and they are also naturally very hard to interpret. Nevertheless, the range 65 of forms in Hawaii is very large; dots and circles which may record childbirths, human figures of various types, dogs, birdmen, canoes, and boards for playing the game of *konane*.[38] Geometric symbols are rare, except for the dots and circles, and most carvings were clearly done individually and were not intended to be parts of scenes. At Puako on Hawaii,

64 A hamlet on Kauai, drawn by John Webber on Cook's third voyage.

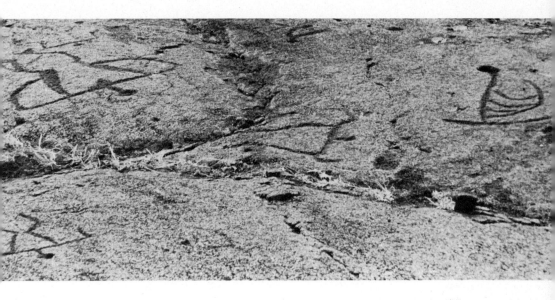

however, there are some unusual processions of humans in lines of up to 29 spreadeagled figures. In the nineteenth century the art of petroglyph carving died out, but not before the production of a few examples of mission-taught writing, and the occasional man on horseback. It may be noted here that petroglyphs and rock-paintings with a fair degree of stylistic unity are found throughout Polynesia, but I will only mention them again in connection with Easter Island and New Zealand.

65 Hawaiian petroglyphs: human figures and a canoe at Pu'uloa, Puna, Hawaii.

## The Mystery Islands

Not all the islands settled by Polynesians had populations at European discovery; I have already mentioned Necker and Nihoa in the Hawaiian Islands, and there are many more. The remarkable fact is that the Polynesians seem to have left some traces on virtually every speck of land within the Polynesian triangle, but whether the abandoned islands were visited purposefully or simply occupied for a time by stray voyagers we shall probably never know.

The Phoenix and Line Islands of equatorial Polynesia are atolls. It is possible that all were visited by Polynesians, although not all have been surveyed archaeologically. Nevertheless, Malden and Fanning Islands both have remains of house floors and possible temples, perhaps related to those of Penrhyn Island in the northern Cooks. Other atolls with traces of settlement include Washington, Christmas, Palmerston, and Suwarrow;

why they were not settled permanently is not known, although some are subject to drought, and others (especially Suwarrow) are very small and subject to hurricane devastation. The Kermadec Islands to the north of New Zealand also have traces of occupation, as does Norfolk Island between New Zealand and New Caledonia.

In the far east of Polynesia lies the most famous mystery island of all – Pitcairn. The Bounty mutineers who settled here in 1790 found coconuts and breadfruit growing, and also stone platforms with statues a little like those on Easter Island.[39] Recent excavations here and on neighbouring Henderson Island suggest that settlement goes back to about 1100, and Pitcairn is a fertile volcanic island which has produced quantities of fishhooks, stone adzes and pig bones, as well as settlement sites and stone quarries. It was clearly settled for quite a long time by a sizeable population whose ultimate fate is unknown. Pitcairn is only about 500 kilometres from Mangareva, so the settlers may have come from here.

It is worth mentioning that many small coral islands in the vicinity of larger settled islands were visited regularly for exploitative purposes, without supporting a permanent population. They are however, in a rather different class from the much more isolated islands described here. Islands in this known and visited class include Nassau near Pukapuka in the northern Cooks, Tetiaroa near Tahiti, and Takutea near Atiu (southern Cooks). The list is very numerous, and some of these islands were inhabited on a more permanent basis from time to time.

# Into southern waters

The Polynesian cultures described so far, with the exception of
Rapa in the Australs, were all situated within the tropics. The
two cultures described in this chapter are situated outside the
tropics, and archaeologically they are of very special interest.
Some of this interest certainly relates to environmental factors,
especially in New Zealand, where a very different economy from
that of the tropical Polynesians was developed between latitudes
34° and 47° south. The end result here was a warlike society
renowned for its art and tattooing, its fine greenstone artefacts,
and its rather splendid earthwork fortifications. Easter Island, at
27° south latitude, is of course much warmer than New Zealand,
but isolation and apparent cultural introversion here led to the
most magnificent assemblage of stone monuments and carvings
ever created in Polynesia.

## Easter Island

Easter Island is the most isolated island in Polynesia; it lies
almost 2000 kilometres from Pitcairn, and almost 4000 from the
coast of Peru and Chile. It has a total length of only 25
kilometres, and is triangular in shape, being built around a
number of extinct volcanic craters, three of which (Rano Aroi,
Rano Kao and Rano Raraku) contain freshwater lakes. Eight-    66
eenth-century voyagers recorded that the inhabitants grew
sweet potatoes, yams, taro, bananas, sugar cane, gourds and the
paper mulberry tree, all of westerly origin apart from the Andean
sweet potato. They also had domestic chickens, but no pigs or
dogs, and coconut and breadfruit would not grow in the
relatively cool climate. In addition, the island had a number of
useful native plants, including a small tree (*Sophora toromiro*)
used for construction and carving, and a lake reed (*Scirpus
riparius* – the *totora*). Most of the native plants are of South
American origin, but they probably spread to the island prior to
the arrival of man, by natural means. The only good candidate

for human transmission from South America is the sweet potato, and I shall return below to the general question of American contacts.

The first European to discover the island was the Dutchman Roggeveen, on Easter Sunday in 1722. Later visitors included a Spanish expedition in 1770, Captain Cook in 1774, and the French navigator La Pérouse in 1786. Unfortunately, none of these early visitors stayed more than a few days owing to the lack of food and water – there are no surface streams on the island at all – and none appears to have had any real grasp of the language. Detailed records were thus very few, and this remained the case until 1862, when about 1000 of the islanders, the greater part of the population at this time, were taken by slavers to Peru. After 900 had died the remainder were repatriated, but only 15 arrived home alive, together with smallpox. By 1877 only 110 people remained alive on the island (although a number were then resident in Tahiti), and since detailed records of the island's culture were not made until after this time it is no wonder that so much information was lost. As a result, the past of Easter Island has taken on an aura of mystery which has allowed a number of ridiculous theories to be published in the past, although the balance has now been redressed by modern archaeology, beginning with Thor Heyerdahl's expedition in 1955,[1] and continuing with work by American archaeologists William Mulloy, William Ayres and Patrick McCoy, and Chilean archaeologist Gonzalo Figueroa (Easter Island was annexed by Chile in 1888).[2]

The accounts of early explorers, despite their brevity, do give some insight into Easter Island society during the eighteenth century. In 1722 the famous statues with their topknots were apparently all standing, and the islanders adopted squatting postures in front of them, evidently for purposes of prayer or supplication. Roggeveen and later visitors all noted how barren the island was; trees were virtually absent, as they are today (except for some recently planted stands of eucalyptus), many people were living in refuge caves in a state of evident hostility, and by 1774 many of the statues had been toppled from their pedestals. By 1863 it seems that all the statues were prostrate, the population had undergone a dramatic decline, and one of the world's strangest cultures had crumbled virtually without record. Just why this should have happened still remains unknown, and it is unlikely that the handful of Europeans who visited the island in the eighteenth century had any overwhelm-

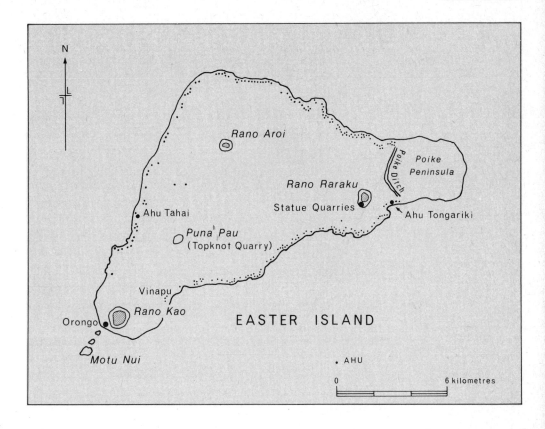

66 The archaeological sites of Easter Island.

ing role in this trend. It seems more likely that environmental degradation coupled with warfare followed the major period of monument and statue construction between AD 1000 and 1600; if the population at this time was as high as 10,000 persons, as McCoy[3] has suggested, then an uncontrolled over-exploitation of resources may well have taken place. The abrupt end to the statue building, to be described below, may also be a notable symptom, and obviously in such an isolated island as Easter any acquisition of new resources through trade or the borrowing of technological innovations was impossible. The island's resources and its population declined hand in hand.

Easter Island society of the eighteenth century was not described as highly stratified, and was dominated by small independent warring tribes who probably spent much of their time fighting over scarce resources. In Goldman's classification (see page 32) Easter was an open society, with the original land-holding ramages being dispersed through frequent warfare and upheaval. However, it does seem likely to me that Easter Island may have been more similar to the societies of Tahiti and Hawaii in its 'Golden Age', and it did have a traditional leading *ariki* line, vested in the Miru family, which may once have wielded a far greater secular power than the nineteenth-century records indicate. The tail end of Easter Island prehistory thus seems rather depressing, but archaeologists have revealed a much more glorious past, to which we now turn.[4]

The linguistic and archaeological evidence pertaining to Easter Island indicates initial settlement around the relatively early date of AD 400–500 from an eastern Polynesian source, perhaps the Marquesas Islands. The island seems to have been completely isolated from other parts of Polynesia after initial settlement, and its material culture lacked the food-pounders and adze styles developed in central Polynesia after AD 1000. In terms of the computer simulation mentioned on page 13 it would be extremely difficult to reach the island from the west anyway, although it would in theory be easier for drifting canoes to run back westwards into Polynesia from an Easter Island starting point. In this respect, we may note that Pitcairn once had a number of stone statues, possibly of Easter Island type (see page 110).

Following the work of the Norwegian expedition led by Thor Heyerdahl to the island in 1955–6, Easter Island prehistory was divided into three periods.[5] The Early Period, from AD 400 to 1100, was characterized by the earliest stone platforms (*ahu*), and during the Middle Period (1100–1680) these platforms were embellished with the haughty and standardized statues for which the island is so famous. Finally, the Late Period (1680–1868) is

67 Cut-stone facing of an undated *ahu* at Hanga Poukura, Easter Island.

characterized by the dramatic decline described above, and it closes with the arrival of Christian missionaries. More recent work has shown that the division between Early and Middle Periods may not be as sharp as once thought, although the Late Period is particularly well marked, and it also comes within the range of fragmentary traditional evidence.

This three-period division is based mainly on the results of excavations of the *ahu*, of which about 300 still remain in surprising density around the rocky and barren coasts of the island. In the Early and Middle Periods the larger *ahu* consisted of rectangular platforms, often very finely faced on their seaward sides, which abutted on their inland sides on to long sloping ramps paved with rows of spaced boulders. These ramps in turn led down into rectangular cleared courts, which were generally unenclosed. The largest recorded *ahu*, called Tongariki (destroyed recently by a tidal wave), had a central platform about 45 metres long, and a total length, with the two wings, of about 160 metres. The central platform supported no fewer than 15 statues during the Middle Period.

A number of *ahu* are known or believed to belong to the Early period, although information is rather scarce. *Ahu* number 2 at Vinapu, possibly built about AD 850, comprised a central

68 Two reconstructed *ahu* near Hangaroa on Easter Island.

67

68

69 Statue with bent knees and beard excavated from the Rano Raraku quarry debris.

platform 36 by 4 metres in area and three metres high, faced with large vertical slabs of rough stone filled and levelled with dry-stone work.[6] This abutted on its inland side on to a long sloping ramp with wings, and beyond this was a cleared court surrounded on two sides by an earthen bank. Another Early period *ahu* is *Ahu* Tahai,[7] one of a cluster of *ahu* recently reconstructed by William Mulloy near the village of Hangaroa, and this was constructed as a similar winged platform about AD 700; the central platform was faced with carefully dressed and fitted blocks of stone, and this is so far the earliest date for the use of dressed stone in Polynesia.

It is not yet clear whether the *ahu* supported statues during the Early Period, and the famous busts quarried at Rano Raraku seem to belong entirely in the Middle Period, after AD 1000–1100. However, fragmentary stone statues have been found re-used as construction material in Middle Period *ahu*, and Heyerdahl's team excavated an unusual statue with bent

knees and a goatee beard at Rano Raraku, which they believed to
belong to the Early Period. The question remains open, but since
the plans of the Easter Island *ahu* are similar to those of simple
*marae* structures in central Polynesia (albeit on a larger scale),
then it would cause no surprise to discover that upright slabs or
small statues were in use in the Early Period. A local origin for
the Middle Period statues from simple forebears does seem
extremely likely.

During the Middle Period many new *ahu* were built, and some
existing ones, such as Vinapu 2 and Tahai, were rebuilt to
support the massive stone busts. These were placed singly or in
rows of up to sixteen, facing inland into the courts, with their
backs towards the sea. About 100 of the *ahu* eventually received
one or more of these statues, which comprise legless busts with
long-fingered hands stretched across their stomachs, and
remarkably standardized facial features. Many also have
elongated ear-lobes, and at least one has disc-shaped ear plugs.

70 Re-erected statues at
*Ahu* Akivi (these appear
never to have had
topknots).

70

71 The quarries of Rano Raraku.

Some 600 of these statues still survive, and over 150 of them remain unfinished in the quarries of Rano Raraku, to which we now turn.

71    The Rano Raraku extinct volcano is composed of a fairly soft andesitic tuff, and the quarries for the statues are located inside and outside the crater rim, right up to the rather precipitous summit.[8] Workmen shaped the statues in the rock with stone

72    mauls until they were almost finished, and attached to the rock only by spines left down their backs. When the spines were severed the statues were lowered by ropes down to the base of the slope, and several large holes still survive in the crater rim where large posts were set to take the ropes. At the bottom of the slope

73    the statues were erected upright and given some finishing touches, apart from the carving of the eyes, which was done on the *ahu* after final erection. This may have been to ensure that the powers which the statues doubtless possessed were not activated until the proper time. However, a number did have their backs embellished at the quarries with symbols which appear to represent loin-cloths and tattooing designs.

After the statues were dressed at the base of the quarries they were then moved along cleared roads to the *ahu* in various parts

74    of the island, to be erected with their dark-red cylindrical topknots which were carved in another volcanic crater called Punapau. William Mulloy has recently suggested that a forked sled was attached to the front of each statue to protect it from contact with the rough ground, and sled and statue were then

72 An unfinished statue 20 m long lying in the Rano Raraku quarries.

73 Statues (virtually buried under slumped quarry debris) awaiting transport from the foot of Rano Raraku.

74 Re-erected statue with topknot at *Ahu* Ku te Riku, near Hangaroa.

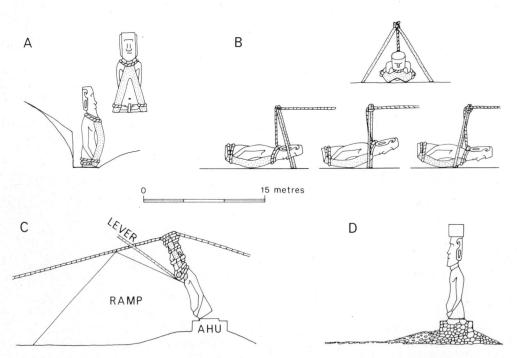

75 Transportation and erection of Easter Island statues, according to William Mulloy: *a* attachment of forked sled; *b* transportation with bipod; *c* erection of statue with topknot lashed to head; *d* erected statue with masonry ramp removed.

slung from the apex of a huge wooden bipod, which was pulled repeatedly through a vertical position, thus moving the statue in a series of hops.[9] When the *ahu* was reached the statue and topknot were lashed together and raised by levers and ramps. According to Mulloy, the largest statue ever erected on the *ahu* (11.5 metres high with topknot and weighing 84 tonnes) would have taken 30 men one year to carve, 90 men two months to move the six kilometres from the quarry, and 90 men three months to erect. Not all the statues actually reached their *ahu*, as a small number of broken and abandoned examples indicate.

75

Other archaeological manifestations of the Middle Period include boat-shaped houses with drilled kerbstones to hold the arched timbers which supported the roof. Circular and rectangular houses were built as well, although the boat-shaped variety is the most characteristic on the island. Sometimes quite large groups of house foundations occur together, and there is one famous village called Orongo, on top of the crater rim of Rano Kao overlooking the sea.[10] The Orongo village consisted of about 48 oval stone houses with corbelled and earth-covered roofs, having narrow entrance tunnels and dark interiors lined

76

76 Boat-shaped house with drilled kerbstones, near *Ahu* Tahai.

77 Rock carvings of birdmen at Orongo.

with upright slabs. The houses are tightly clustered in lines and around plazas, and one room contained a statue of *ahu* type made of a hard rock which does not occur on Rano Raraku. On the rocks near the village are many carvings of bird-headed 77 humanoid figures, some clutching eggs. These may have represented Makemake, the Easter Island god of creation, and evidently the patron of this ceremony.

Every year, members of the tribal groups in military ascendance gathered at Orongo, and each appointed a servant to 78 swim with a reed float to the small island of Motu Nui, about 1.5 kilometres off the south-western tip of the main island. Here, the servants awaited the arrival of migratory sooty terns, which laid their eggs on the island. The first servant to find an egg called out to watchers on the mainland, and his master was placed in *tapu* seclusion for several months in a special house near Rano Raraku, apparently as a representative of Makemake. Fortunately this ceremony continued until 1867, and thus survived to be recorded. However, we do not know whether the ceremony in this form actually goes back to the Middle Period, although carbon-14 dates indicate that the Orongo village itself was constructed around AD 1500.

78 The island of Motu
Nui (furthest from
camera). Birdmen are
carved on the rocks in the
foreground.

All this evidence for the carving and erection of statues, *ahu*, and masonry houses suggests that during the Middle Period a comparative peace reigned on the island, with the members of different tribal groups doing the work at the behest of their chiefs. Although there is no good evidence that the island was ever under a single ruler, the remarkable degree of island-wide standardization in statues and *ahu* plans could suggest that this was the case. George Forster also recorded in 1774 that the statues represented deceased chiefs, and if this was so then these personages may have attained a prestige unparalleled in other parts of Polynesia.

Whatever the answers, it is clear that the whole system was in decline by perhaps as early as 1600. Statue carving had apparently finished by this time, and the unfinished statues left standing at the quarry base or still attached to the rock indicate that the end was short and dramatic. One unfinished 20-metre giant does suggest that ambition was exceeding technology at the end of the Middle Period; it is hard to see how such a huge statue could have been erected if ever it were finished. Also, loss of the island's timber would have made movement of the statues very difficult, and internecine warfare was developing too – both on

72

79 Toppled statues on *Ahu* Akahanga, Late Period.

79

80

81

82

the evidence of the tradition of a war between the enigmatic 'Long Ears' and 'Short Ears' around 1680, and on the evidence of the many obsidian spearheads found exclusively in Late Period sites. As we saw above, all the statues were toppled by 1863, and this tragedy can only have reflected a social upheaval of enormous magnitude. The *ahu* with their toppled statues were piled up with small stones into which cists were built for human burials, and the original functions of the *ahu* were gradually forgotten.

The increasing lack of timber and the probable decline in security are also reflected in the dwellings and allied structures of the Late Period. Cave dwellings built into the fissured and pocketed lava flows become very common, and these were sometimes lined with walls made from blocks taken from *ahu* and boat-shaped house foundations. Also of probable Late Period date are the tall stone towers with internal corbelled chambers, known as *tupa*. These might have functioned as fortified dwellings, although I think this is unlikely since all are in exposed coastal situations, and their functions in fact remain unknown.

The artefacts of both the Middle and Late Periods (few are known from the Early Period) form a homogeneous group of basic Polynesian type; stone adzes, bait fishhooks of bone and stone (but no lure hooks), stone bowls, obsidian flakes and tanged spearheads, and several minor categories including

80 Late Period burial cist constructed in the rubble of a destroyed image *ahu*.

81 A *tupa*, with a corbelled room inside.

82 Obsidian spearhead (*mataa*), 9 cm long. Late Period.

grindstones and basalt knives. None of these artefact types have South American antecedents, and the important Andean categories of pottery, metalwork, and pressure-flaked stone tools are absent, as are the important domesticated plants, maize, beans and squashes. The statues do have unique features, but it is not hard to derive them from other widespread Polynesian forms in stone and wood. Other features sometimes claimed to have American antecedents, such as corbelled roofs, birdman symbols and double-bladed paddles, are either well paralleled elsewhere in Polynesia and other parts of the Pacific, or so simple that a local development can hardly be disputed.

The question of American contacts is of course an important one, especially for Easter Island, on which the views of Thor Heyerdahl are now so well known. As explained on page 19, Heyerdahl believed that Caucasoids from the Tiahuanaco region of Bolivia preceded the Polynesians in Polynesia, and after his expedition to Easter Island (which was without doubt a masterpiece of organization and research), he suggested this island was first settled by Tiahuanaco peoples with sun-worship and the worship of Makemake. At the end of the Early Period he felt that the island was abandoned, but resettled by fresh groups

83

from South America in the Middle Period with the birdman cult and the ancestor memorial cult represented by the statues. These people were then wiped out by the Polynesians who arrived from British Columbia later in the Middle Period.

83 (*opposite*) A wooden birdman carving (*tangata menu*), 26 cm long. Probably of nineteenth-century date.

After the passage of 20 years since Heyerdahl published his ideas,[11] it is clear that there is no evidence, linguistic or

84 The seaward face of *ahu* number 1 at Vinapu. Compare the small insert at right with that shown in Figure 85.

85 (*below*) Masonry inserts at Sacsayhuaman, Cuzco, Peru. Fifteenth century.

archaeological, which can be used to support a major American settlement on the island, or anywhere else in Polynesia. On the other hand there is the sweet potato, with its Polynesian name *kumara*, similar to the term *kumar* used by some Quechua tribes of Peru.[12] Furthermore, the *ahu* number 1 at Vinapu was probably constructed at the end of the Middle Period, about AD 1500,[13] and its superb face of precisely fitted stone blocks is so similar to contemporary Peruvian Inca masonry that I feel some limited contact did take place about this time. However, it should be pointed out that Vinapu 1 is the only *ahu* of this type

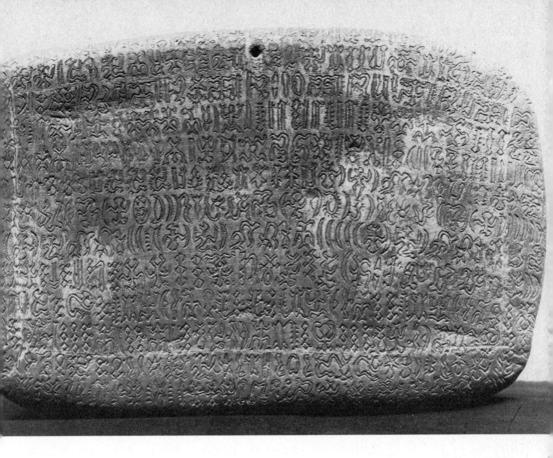

out of some 300 on the island, and it doubtless represents no
more than the chance arrival of a raft-load of Peruvian Indians
acquainted with Inca techniques of construction. Otherwise, as a
Peruvian specialist has recently indicated,[14] the evidence for
American contact is slim indeed, and wind and current patterns
along the Peruvian coast would make frequent arrivals most
unlikely.

Finally, we have the well-known script of Easter Island,
known as *rongorongo*, carved in the reversed boustrophedon
fashion alternatively from right to left and left to right on small
wooden boards. This script was not reported by anyone before
1864, and some of the boards are of timbers foreign to the island
and certainly post-European in origin. The script itself has about
120 elements, many based on birdman or human symbols, and it
has never been satisfactorily deciphered; the Peruvian slave-
raids evidently removed all persons with the requisite knowledge. Barthel[15] thinks that the script was basically ideographic
rather than pictographic, and that some of the symbols had
phonetic values as well. It may have been used to record chants
and genealogical data, although Métraux[16] believed that the

86 A wooden *rongorongo*
tablet, now in the Santiago
Museum, Chile.

86

129

symbols were simply pictographic and used as mnemonic aids during chanting. Some of the symbols are also found in petroglyphs on the island, and some were drawn by islanders on an annexation document drawn up by a Spanish expedition in 1770. However, there is no sign of the script in its over-all form in any prehistoric context, and I would agree with Emory[17] that it is of post-European but indigenous inspiration, perhaps developed between 1770 and 1864. It would be exciting if future work could prove this view wrong, for we would then be faced with the only authentic example of a prehistoric script to be developed anywhere in Oceania.

## New Zealand

The two large islands of New Zealand (North Island and South Island) present a prehistoric sequence which is unique in the Polynesian context. They are larger than the rest of Polynesia put together (over 250,000 square kilometres), and they have a climate which trends from warm temperate in the north to cool temperate in the south. There are perhaps few countries in the world of similar size which have such a degree of environmental variation, ranging from active volcanoes, high alpine fold mountains, inland lakes and plains, and a highly dissected and varied coastline – the latter being especially important from the viewpoint of the first settlers. The consensus of modern opinion is that these first settlers were the lineal ancestors of the present Maori people, and that they arrived towards the end of the first millennium AD. New Zealand was evidently the last major region of Polynesia to be settled.

87

While the small tropical islands of Polynesia each supported fairly homogeneous societies in terms of economy and language, the same cannot be said of New Zealand. The Maori language was divided into a number of dialects at contact, albeit not markedly divergent, but the economy showed regional differences of a major order,[18] comparable to those in the northern temperate regions of Europe. By far the greater part of the eighteenth-century Maori population lived around the warm coastal fringes of the North Island, especially in the northern half; here they could grow sweet potatoes and limited quantities of yams, taro and gourds, and they also had plentiful sources of edible fern rhizomes. Horticulture rapidly dwindled in importance in the southern half of the North Island and the northern half of the South, and the peoples of the greater part of the South

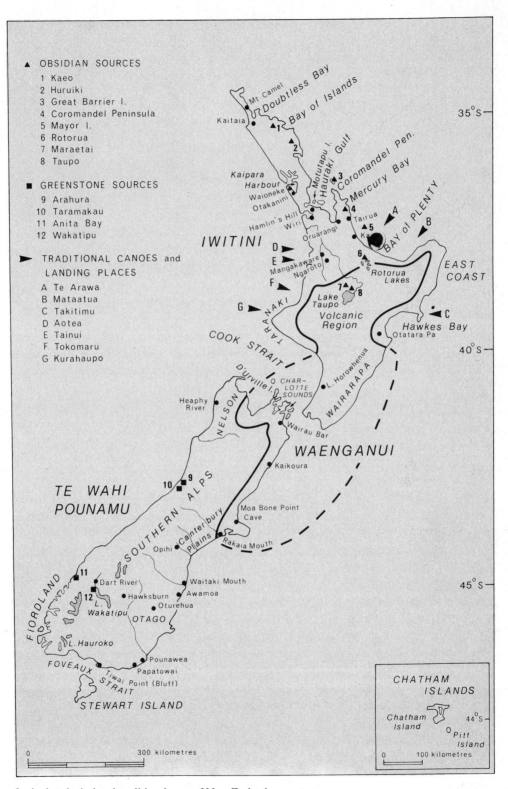

**OBSIDIAN SOURCES**
1 Kaeo
2 Huruiki
3 Great Barrier I.
4 Coromandel Peninsula
5 Mayor I.
6 Rotorua
7 Maraetai
8 Taupo

**GREENSTONE SOURCES**
9 Arahura
10 Taramakau
11 Anita Bay
12 Wakatipu

**TRADITIONAL CANOES and**
**LANDING PLACES**
A Te Arawa
B Mataatua
C Takitimu
D Aotea
E Tainui
F Tokomaru
G Kurahaupo

87 Archaeological and traditional map of New Zealand.

Island and the Chatham Islands were completely unable to practise horticulture with the available crops; they lived entirely by birding, fishing and gathering. The population gradient from north to south was extremely steep in the eighteenth century, although, as we shall see below, this was certainly not the case in the early days of settlement.

Although the first settlers brought a number of tropical food crops with them (doubtless unsuccessfully in the cases of coconut, banana and breadfruit) together with the dog, they did from the beginning have the advantage of a number of native food sources. The podocarp forests of the North Island and the eastern half of the South supported large bird populations, including the flightless moa which was rapidly hunted to extinction.[19] Shellfish were particularly plentiful, especially in estuarine mud-flat situations, and the native fern rhizome (*Pteridium esculentum*) was quickly brought into semi-cultivation, and throughout prehistory was probably more important than the sweet potato in terms of yield.[20] The introduced crops, of which the sweet potato was the most successful, needed rather special care, and in the New Zealand climate would only produce one crop in the warmer months of the year. The sweet potato also required friable soils which had to be aerated artificially with many tonnes of gravel in some regions, and it also required a complicated type of winter storage, which I shall describe later. By 1770 the New Zealand economy was supporting between 100,000 and 150,000 people,[21] of whom perhaps 80 per cent lived in the warmer coastal fringes of the North Island.

The origins of the Maori have never been established with certainty, but archaeological and linguistic considerations make the Cook and Society Islands the most likely, and Green and Sinoto[22] have also raised the possibility of a Marquesan settlement. But even if the exact source is not now traceable, owing to cultural convergence in eastern Polynesia as one goes back in time, the evidence of a source within these three groups is almost irrefutable. Earlier theories of Melanesian or western Polynesian settlements in New Zealand have not withstood recent examination.

The prehistoric sequence in New Zealand is normally divided into two periods or phases; Roger Duff, in his major work first published in 1950,[23] organized the material into an earlier Moa-hunter period and a later Maori period, and Jack Golson in 1959[24] modified this into the terminology most widely used

88 (*opposite*) The New Zealand Archaic assemblage (from various sites).

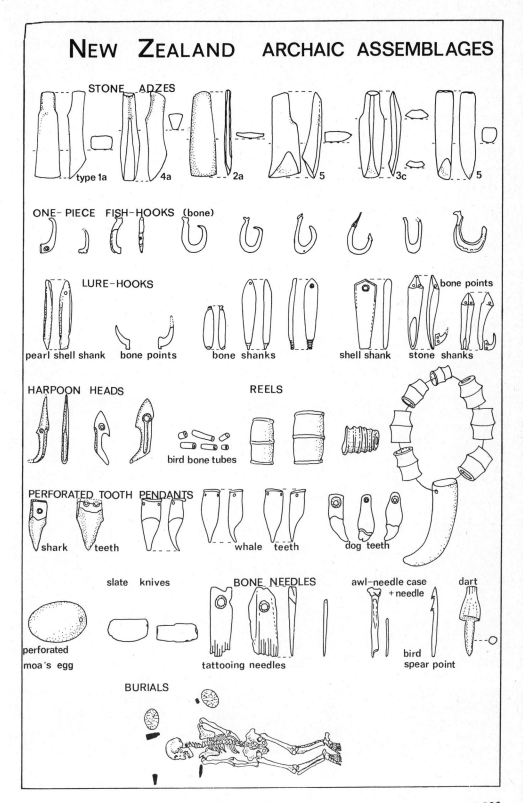

# NEW ZEALAND ARCHAIC ASSEMBLAGES

**STONE ADZES**

type 1a        4a        2a        5        3c        5

**ONE-PIECE FISH-HOOKS (bone)**

**LURE-HOOKS**

bone points

pearl shell shank        bone points        bone shanks        shell shank        stone shanks

**HARPOON HEADS**        **REELS**

bird bone tubes

**PERFORATED TOOTH PENDANTS**

shark    teeth        whale    teeth        dog teeth

slate    knives        **BONE NEEDLES**        awl-needle case        dart
                                              + needle

perforated
moa's egg        tattooing needles        bird
                                          spear point

**BURIALS**

today. Golson coined the term 'New Zealand Eastern Polynesian Culture' for the whole sequence, and divided this into an earlier Archaic phase and a later Classic (or classic Maori) phase. In the North Island the Archaic lasts from initial settlement to around AD 1350, and is then followed by the major Classic developments which run through to European contact. The South Island remained in the Archaic phase throughout its prehistory. These divisions mean that the terms Archaic and Classic do not refer to over-all time divisions; hence Golson's preference for the term 'phase' with its cultural connotations rather than 'period', which has more of a chronological orientation.

## The Archaic phase

The Archaic phase witnessed the settlement of the whole of New Zealand by settlers with a characteristically Early Eastern

89 Pair of chevroned amulets of whale ivory from Aniseed, Kaikoura, South Island. The right-hand example is 149 mm long.

90 The wooden carving
from Kaitaia, of presumed
Archaic style. Length
1.7 m.

Polynesian material culture (see page 63). The spread was apparently very rapid, and so far there are no indications where the first settlers might have landed, since sites going back to about AD 1000 have been found from north to south throughout the coastal regions of the country. The greatest densities of both human and moa populations seem to have occurred down the eastern coast of the South Island, and this is where the largest and richest sites have so far been found, especially at the Wairau Bar site mentioned on page 63. The artefact types listed there for Wairau represent virtually the whole range reported from the New Zealand Archaic prior to AD 1350, with the notable exception of the rather enigmatic 'chevroned amulets' of whale ivory,[25] found widely in the South Island and believed on stylistic grounds to predate the Classic Maori art style. A wooden carving from a swamp at Kaitaia in the North Island, perhaps a roof ornament for a storehouse, also possesses this characteristic angularity and is considered Archaic. With the exception of these specimens and the rock-art to be described later, we really know very little about Archaic Maori art.

Most of the large South Island Archaic sites are found, expectably, near the mouths of rivers. One of the largest known covers about 60 hectares with occupation deposits at the mouth of the Waitaki River in Otago; Wairau Bar itself is reported to cover between six and eight hectares. However, it is most unlikely that such large areas were ever utilized contemporaneously, and they are more likely to represent palimpsests of many successive seasons of occupation in a general locality. Since these large sites were excavated before the use of modern archaeological techniques, we are rather lacking in precise information. Nevertheless, the South Island economy was basically non-horticultural, and this circumstance led to a

88

89

90

pattern of seasonal movement which is recorded ethnographically and in recent archaeological analyses; the coastal sites may
represent winter camps, while the population perhaps split into
smaller groups in the summer, and some of these groups moved
inland. At Oturehua in central Otago small groups were
exploiting a local quartzite for stone tools, perhaps on a seasonal
basis, from about AD 1100.[26] With one or two exceptions,[27]
settlement patterns within the South Island sites remain
unknown, and most reports indicate little more than the spread
of an occupation deposit containing charcoal, shellfish, food
bones and artefacts.

   The North Island sites, like those in the South, also have
mainly a coastal distribution, although there is limited evidence
for inland occupation in the Waikato and Lake Taupo regions.[28]
An analysis by Shawcross of the remains excavated at a camp
called Mount Camel, at the mouth of the Houhora Harbour near
the northern tip of the North Island, has provided perhaps the
most detailed information on any Archaic site known in New
Zealand.[29] The Mount Camel site covered about 1.5 hectares
(quite small by eastern South Island standards), and was situated
91  on a platform a little above high-water mark. The area excavated
(about 100 square metres) was associated with a cluster of earth-
ovens, and evidence for butchering, fish scaling, cooking,
fishhook manufacture, and the manufacture of bone and ivory
ornaments. The artefact assemblage, dating to between AD 1150
and 1260 approximately, contained many one-piece fishhooks of
bone, adzes of Archaic type, and ornaments including reels,
whale teeth, and tubes of bird bone. Trolling hook shanks,
harpoons and tattooing chisels were also present.

   The economic analysis was undertaken on some 21,000 bones
of fish, seal, dolphin, dog, rat and moa. Shellfish were of little
importance, although they could have been eaten at seasonal
camps elsewhere. Some of the fish were also dressed on the site
and their bodies taken and eaten elsewhere, while the moas seem
to have been dressed at kill sites and brought back to Mount
Camel without their lower legs. The large sizes of one species of
fish (*Chrysophrys auratus*, the snapper) also indicated that the
inhabitants were exploiting a population not previously
exploited heavily by man, and they evidently fed many of the
smaller ones to dogs, to judge from an analysis of coprolites.
From a reconstruction of the meat weights represented by the
bones of the various food species it appears that seals provided
the most meat, while fish were the most numerous as individuals.

91 The Mount Camel
Archaic site, Northland.
The site is marked by the
grid of excavation trenches
in the middle distance
(the quarry behind
is modern).

Shawcross finally suggests that the food remains recovered indicate that a family of five individuals could have utilized the site for about twelve six-month seasons.

Without more analyses of the Mount Camel type it is difficult to say just how representative this site is of Archaic economy; environmental differences throughout the country probably led to considerable variation in population density and spacing, despite the evident degree of cultural homogeneity prior to AD 1300. The largest human populations may well have co-existed with the largest moa populations in the eastern South Island, but the North Island also raises the important question of the development of horticulture.

Until quite recently, it was felt that the Archaic phase throughout New Zealand was completely non-horticultural.[30] This view has now been changed by a limited number of finds; horticultural soils for taro or sweet potato have been claimed for Archaic contexts in the Bay of Islands and the Wairarapa district,[31] and a site called Skipper's Ridge on the Coromandel Peninsula has produced rectangular storage pits for sweet potatoes going back to the twelfth century.[32] The evidence is slight, and horticulture was perhaps not as important as it was to become in the Classic phase in the North Island, but the plants may indeed have been brought by the first settlers. Faced with a bounteous and unexploited natural environment they perhaps felt unwilling to engage in the labour of clearing and weeding gardens until the changing balance of resources persuaded them to do so.

Since New Zealand straddles the edge of the climatic range of sweet potato the plant could only be grown seasonally, and had to be stored through the winter in rectangular underground pits. In Classic sites in the North Island these pits are very common, and were normally roofed and covered with a thick layer of soil to maintain inside temperatures above 5° C and relatively high humidity. Bell-shaped pits with small surface openings were also used. The rarity of these pits in the Archaic may suggest the unimportance of horticulture, as noted above, but it may also reflect an important climatic factor. It is becoming increasingly clear that the climate during the Archaic phase in New Zealand was warmer than now, and it may have been warm enough for pit storage to be unnecessary in some regions;[33] hence rarity of pits in Archaic sites may not necessarily mean absence of horticulture, although this is a problem for future research to resolve. It appears that a climatic deterioration set in around AD 1300–1400, and this is especially clear in the Wairarapa district at the southern end of the North Island – an area which was generally too cold for horticulture in the Classic phase, but which has produced extensive roughly rectangular field systems of Archaic date, bounded by low walls of stones removed from the soil.[34] After 1400 the climate in this district became more rugged, and deforestation and erosion set in, leading to an apparent cessation of horticulture. In the warmer regions to the north the consequences of this change were not so drastic, and the horticultural systems were evidently saved by the increased use of pit storage through the cold winters. This extremely important development possibly lies partly at the base of the success and spread of Classic Maori culture, as we shall see below.

Another very interesting aspect of New Zealand prehistory not found in the smaller tropical islands of Polynesia is the long-distance trade in various lithic resources for tool-making. This certainly begins in the earliest Archaic sites, and is associated with a number of rock sources. Good flaking obsidian was traded throughout New Zealand from a source on Mayor Island in the Bay of Plenty, and another source near Lake Taupo was in use in

107

the Archaic as well (see locations on figure 87). The fabled resources of greenstone (nephrite) in the valleys of the Taramakau and Arahura Rivers in Westland were probably exploited in limited fashion in the Archaic, although these only attained major importance in the Classic. Argillites for adze-making were also traded throughout the country from sources in Nelson and on D'Urville Island, and quartzites from several Otago sites were traded locally. Nowhere is there evidence for a full-time group of traders, and these products were apparently exchanged in limited quantities between adjacent groups.

In the North Island, the change from Archaic to Classic is most conveniently dated to around AD 1350, although the break is by no means sharp, and to my mind is characterized mainly by the appearance of earthwork fortifications, and an apparent sharp increase in the importance of pit storage for sweet potato. Artefact styles change more gradually, as we shall see below. In the South Island the Archaic life-style as represented by small mobile groups survives with relatively minor changes in artefact types to the period of European contact. The only exception occurs in the northern and north-eastern coastal regions, where Classic Maori immigrants (the Ngai Tahu tribe) settled from the eastern North Island around 1550, according to traditional and archaeological evidence.

Over most of the South Island the population perhaps reached a peak in the period between 1200 and 1400,[35] although the forest cover and moa populations were certainly under pressure by this time, leading to a greater concentration on marine resources, including sea mammals. After 1500 the population apparently declined quite markedly, and many inland sites, especially the ones with rock-art (see below) were no longer visited. By 1769 the South Island was for the most part only thinly peopled – partly due to destruction of forest cover in the eastern regions[36] – and its Archaic role as perhaps the most densely settled part of the country was sadly reversed. The enforced absence of horticulture was clearly a negative stimulus to this development, since the North Island witnessed a contemporary and unparalleled phase of population growth and cultural change.

The gradual demise of South Island population and economy is revealed in the history of the rock-art so well preserved on cliffs, overhangs and rock-shelters in the limestone regions of Canterbury and Otago.[37] Perhaps 95 per cent of the four hundred or so art sites recorded in New Zealand are in these

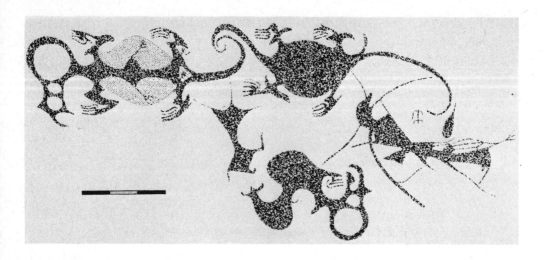

92
92 The charcoal-drawn 'taniwha' at Opihi, south Canterbury. (Scale is in feet.)

regions, and the motifs themselves are drawn with dry pigments, generally in red (hematite) or black (charcoal). The designs are quite homogeneous, and include dogs, birds (including moa) and fish, together with mythical creatures generally called *taniwha*. The drawings can be simply outlined, or partly or completely filled in with pigment, and the animals may be portrayed in side-on or spreadeagled poses. This art has generic parallels in other parts of Polynesia, especially in the Hawaiian Islands, and there is no sign of any extra-Polynesian influence. Most excavated occupation deposits in the shelters indicate activity between 1000 and 1500, and after this time the sites seem to have been abandoned as the decreasing population came to depend more and more on marine resources.

To close this section on the Archaic, mention should be made of the Chatham Islands, 900 km east of Christchurch. When discovered in 1791 these islands supported a population of about 2000 people,[38] living entirely by hunting, fishing and gathering. This group was evidently settled from New Zealand during the Archaic phase, and thereafter virtually isolated, so that the eighteenth-century population had developed a rather different language known as Moriori. Most of the New Zealand Archaic artefact types are present on the island, including adzes, reel and whale-tooth ornaments, harpoons, and baited fishhooks (trolling hooks were absent). Simple hand-clubs of *patu* type are also quite common. As in the South Island, this assemblage apparently underwent local development until European contact, but economic change in the absence of horticulture, and also of a moa population, was perhaps limited. Present

93

archaeological work in the group from the University of Otago should improve this rather sparse picture. However, the Chathams are of potential interest, since they represent the only truly isolated population of non-horticultural Polynesians. They were indeed among the most isolated peoples of the prehistoric world.

93 Stone *patu* type clubs and a tanged spearhead (compare figure 82) from the Chatham Islands. Left-hand specimen is 32 cm long.

## The Classic Maori phase in the North Island

The Classic Maori developments occur in the North Island and the north-eastern fringes of the South, and are closely correlated geographically with the distribution of sweet potato cultivation. This circumstance is clearly not coincidence, and while the sweet

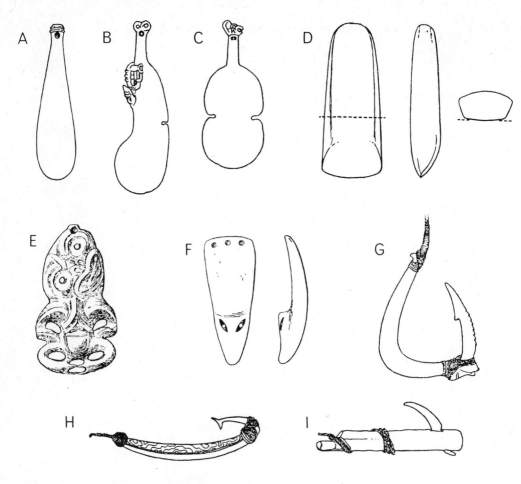

94 Artefacts of Classic Maori type (not to scale): a–c hand-clubs of stone or whalebone: *patu*, *wahaika* and *kotiate* respectively; *d* adze of Duff type 2B; *e* greenstone (nephrite) *hei tiki*; *f* whale tooth pendant (*rei puta*); *g* two-piece bait hook with wooden shank and bone point; *h Kahawai* lure, with *Haliotis* shell strip on wooden shank, and point of bone; *i* barracuda lure with wooden shank and bone point.

potato may not have produced an over-all annual yield equal to that from the fern rhizome, it nevertheless provided a very major edge in productivity over the non-horticultural areas of the South Island. The fern rhizome itself also seems to have been more productive in the north, although reliable data to quantify this statement are lacking.

As noted above, the Classic phase is characterized by fortifications, pit storage, and new artefact types, all undergoing a fairly sharp development after 1350. These changes are accompanied by increases in population, warfare, and settlement size. The Classic Maori phase, to my mind, represents not merely cultural change, but an onset of quite dramatic cultural evolution, in some ways comparable to that from Neolithic to Iron Age in Britain.

The Classic Maori assemblage does not, of course, represent a total break from the Archaic; many of the changes perhaps took place over several centuries, and since artefacts made of organic materials (such as wood) have so rarely survived from the Archaic we are obliged to restrict observations to those made of stone or bone. Nevertheless, by 1500 a fairly homogeneous cultural assemblage[39] had spread through the North Island, and this assemblage shows marked differences in most respects from that of the Archaic.

94

Classic adzes, for instance, are entirely of the tangless Duff type 2B, and the earlier variety represented at sites such as Wairau Bar disappears completely. One-piece bait hooks for fishing are replaced almost entirely by two-piece forms (also in the South Island), and harpoons and the Archaic types of trolling hooks disappear, to be replaced by the *kahawai* hook in the North Island, and the 'barracuda lure' in the South. The Archaic reels and whale-tooth ornaments also disappear, to be replaced by pendants, for the most part worn singly; the whale-tooth *rei puta* and the greenstone *hei tiki* were both popular at European contact. New weapon types appear as well, particularly the *kotiate* and *wahaika* varieties of hand-club, and the numerous staff-weapons recorded ethnographically. The simple hand-clubs generally called *patu* do, however, have Archaic forebears, and are also found at the Early Eastern Polynesian site of Vaitootia in the Society Islands (see page 61). They are also present in the Chathams and Easter Island, and are certainly an early form, despite earlier views that warfare was absent in the Archaic.[40]

93

A very large range of wooden artefacts is also known from the Classic Phase, especially from ethnographic collections in museums and from discoveries in swamps and lakes. Some of the lake and swamp finds have been particularly interesting, especially the large collection of combs excavated by Shawcross from a swamp close to the fort at Kauri Point in the Bay of Plenty.[41] Pieces of 187 specimens were recovered, and these had been deposited in a small plank-lined enclosure together with many pieces of obsidian, perhaps used for scarification or hair cutting. In Maori belief the head was sacred, hence the careful deposition of artefacts associated with it. Other Classic assemblages discovered in the bed of Lake Horowhenua near Levin and Lake Mangakaware in the Waikato[42] include a wide range of utilitarian tools; horticultural implements, bowls, weapons, paddles and canoes, palisade posts and house timbers, burial chests, adze and chisel handles, children's tops, and fern rhizome beaters, to list only a few of the more common

95

95 Wooden comb from Kauri Point, Tauranga, 8 cm wide. The nostril is represented by a small head and the mouth contains a small creature, recognizable by the hands.

categories. It is likely that many of these 'everyday' artefact types will also prove to be present in the Archaic, should suitable waterlogged deposits be discovered.

The question now arises of how and why the Classic developments took place. No one has yet solved this problem to the satisfaction of all archaeologists working in New Zealand, and one difficulty is that no sites excavated to date have shown a stratified development from Archaic to Classic. My own view is that the story begins with the adverse climatic change mentioned above; this clearly had a heavy impact on Archaic horticulture in the Wairarapa, and presumably elsewhere in the North Island. If certain groups, perhaps on the Coromandel Peninsula and in Northland, made the fortunate decision to experiment and perfect the rather difficult technique of pit storage for sweet potato, then these groups could maintain and develop their horticulture, while others, especially in the southern half of the North Island, were faced with a horticultural demise. I would suggest that a demographic advantage developed in favour of the Northland and Coromandel regions, to be followed by migrations to the south and conquest, in order to occupy land previously cleared by weaker groups (as hypothesized in more detail by L. M. Groube[43]). The Classic assemblage is so homogeneous that development and spread from a region of fairly limited extent does seem more likely than independent and coincidental development in several places.

This hypothesis does receive some support from Maori traditions. In 1956, Andrew Sharp[44] suggested that the so-called 'Fleet' traditions which form such an important part of Maori oral history referred to population movements within New Zealand, rather than from an outside source in tropical Polynesia as was once believed (see figure 87 for canoe locations). More recently, Groube[45] and Simmons[46] have carried this idea much further, by suggesting that the Fleet traditions actually refer to migrations from Northland to the coastal regions of the North Island, especially Taranaki and the Bay of Plenty. Both Simmons and Groube trace these migrations through the spread of specific types of fortification, which I shall describe later, and date the movements to the period between 1300 and 1500. This period is the one involved in the Fleet genealogies themselves, and it is also the period of expansion of Classic Maori culture and fortifications. Classic Maori art, with its distinctive curvilinear elements not found elsewhere in Polynesia, can also be drawn into the discussion at this point. Mead[47] has recently suggested that this developed within New Zealand from an earlier Archaic style with zoned non-curvilinear decoration similar to the art of other parts of Polynesia and to the decoration of Lapita pottery. He sees the change as a validator, perhaps conscious, of the new social order and patterns of land ownership present in the Classic Maori phase, and his view may perhaps be used to support the above suggestions of population expansion. Classic Maori art is naturally known mostly from ethnographic rather than archaeological collections, and it is particularly renowned for the curvilinear ornamentation applied to facial tattoos, and to wooden items such as canoe prows and sterns, house posts and other building elements, and finely carved feather boxes. For 96, 97 stylistic details the reader is referred to a number of more specialized sources.[48]

97 Carved wooden feather box showing details of Maori surface carving.
Collected on Cook's first voyage (1769). Drawn by R. Ralph.

96 (*opposite*) Maori trophy-head with facial tattoos. Early nineteenth
century. Compare Figure 8.

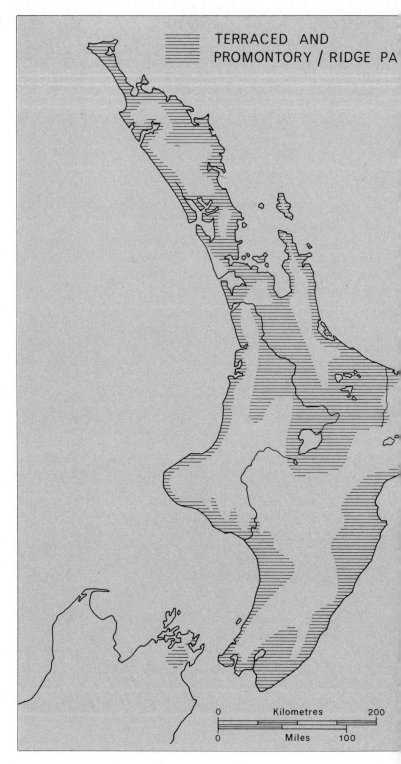

TERRACED AND
PROMONTORY / RIDGE PA

98 Distribution of *pa*
types in the North Island.

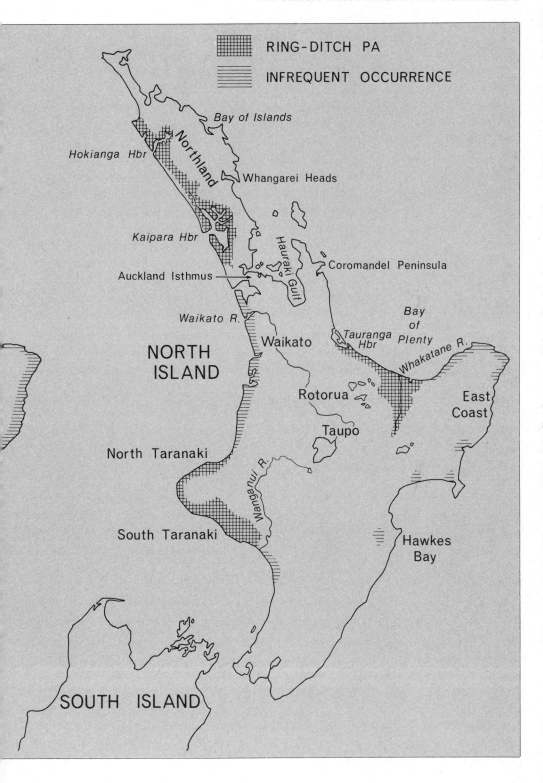

RING-DITCH PA

INFREQUENT OCCURRENCE

Bay of Islands

Northland

Hokianga Hbr

Whangarei Heads

Kaipara Hbr

Hauraki Gulf

Coromandel Peninsula

Auckland Isthmus

Waikato R.

Waikato

Bay of Plenty

Tauranga Hbr

Whakatane R.

NORTH ISLAND

Rotorua

East Coast

Taupo

North Taranaki

Wanganui R.

South Taranaki

Hawkes Bay

SOUTH ISLAND

## The Classic Maori life-style

The major sites in the Classic settlement pattern were the fortifications, called *pa* in Maori, and these functioned in combination with a range of undefended smaller sites such as hamlets, sweet potato storage magazines, and coastal shell-middens. Although some *pa* in favourable environmental regions may have been occupied throughout the year, a pattern of seasonal movement, especially in the summer months, was always characteristic of Maori economy. This is one factor which serves to differentiate Maori from tropical Polynesian economy, even in the regions of highest horticultural development.

98

According to Groube,[49] there are perhaps between 4000 and 6000 *pa* in New Zealand, the majority in the northern half of the North Island. There are no prehistoric *pa* in the South Island beyond the range of sweet potato cultivation. Areas of these sites range from 0.1 to 50 hectares, and densities may be between 1 and 1.5 per square kilometre in the most favourable areas. Groube classifies *pa* into three groups on style of defence: *pa* with terraces only; promontory or ridge *pa* with short transverse ditches; and ring-ditch *pa*. The last are in appearance most like the Iron Age hill forts of southern England, although they are for the most part very much smaller.[50]

99 An aerial view of the terraced *pa* on the extinct volcanic cone of One Tree Hill, Auckland. (White's Aviation photo.)

The terraced *pa* are best developed around the outer slopes of extinct volcanic cones, and several quite large and spectacular ones still survive in the Auckland region, and also in the Bay of Islands. As a class these *pa* may have originated before the others, although the evidence is rather slim. Excavations on the terraces of these *pa*, especially in Auckland, have produced storage pits and some traces of houses, and some may have had palisades along their outer edges, according to drawings of *pa* (not strictly of this class) surviving from the late eighteenth century. Certainly, these sites do not appear to have been strongly fortified by ditches, but their higher sectors probably did have a high potential for defence. Their large size, their apparently limited defences, and the relative lack of extensive excavation on such sites makes them hard to explain.

The promontory and ridge forts form the most common class, and the rather steep terrain of New Zealand provided plentiful opportunities for such constructions. They are generally small, and more obviously designed for defence than the *pa* with terraces only. It should be mentioned here that these *pa*, as well as the ring-ditch type to be described, often have terraces within,

100 A promontory *pa* in the Bay of Islands, with a raised fighting stage shown in use. Drawn by Sydney Parkinson on Cook's first voyage.

100

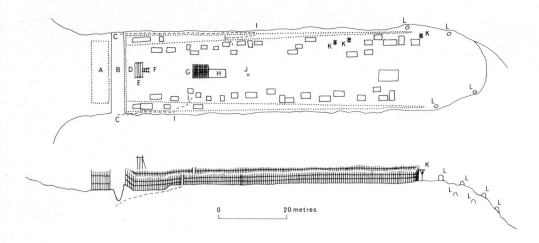

101 101 Plan and side view of a promontory *pa* in the Bay of Islands, made in 1772 during the visit of Marion Du Fresne: *a* outer palisaded work; *b* dry ditch; *c* entrance paths; *d* rampart; *e* fighting stage; *f* ladder to fighting stage; *g* weapon rack; *h* chief's house and weapon store; *i* gates; *j* 'stake having a very hideous head in the shape of a box'; *k* racks for drying fern rhizomes; *l* small houses for storing nets and provisions. The original map also refers to latrines.

and are differentiated from the first group (*pa* with terraces only) by topography and the use of ditches and inner banks.

In 1769 a *pa* of promontory type in Mercury Bay on the Coromandel Peninsula was visited by Cook and Banks,[51] and their descriptions are perhaps the most complete surviving for any prehistoric habitation site in New Zealand. The site was defended across the inland side of the narrow promontory by a bank and ditch eight metres in total height, and by a second outer ditch. Palisades were constructed on the bank and between the two ditches, and just inside the inner palisade were two raised wooden platforms ten metres high for defenders to climb in order to throw spears and stones at an enemy. New Zealand warfare lacked the bow and sling (although these were present in tropical Polynesia), so exposure on these stages was not as dangerous as it might seem. A narrow entrance passage to hamper attackers also passed under one of the stages. Within these defences lay the village, palisaded around the edge of the promontory, and divided internally into 20 separately palisaded dwelling areas, with between one and fourteen houses, many constructed on artificial terraces where the ground was sloping. Quantities of fern rhizomes and dried fish were observed stored inside the *pa*, and part of the interior was planted with gourds and sweet potatoes. Unfortunately, none of the sunken storage pits for sweet potato were reported, and indeed these structures are known only from archaeological excavations, and were never reported by early explorers.

Another *pa* belonging to the promontory class in the Bay of Islands was described by Lieutenant Roux on the expedition of Marion Du Fresne in 1772.[52] Fortunately, a map was made of

102 Ring-ditch *pa* with
double defences at Kauri
Point, Tauranga, Bay of
Plenty.

the site at the time; this shows a rectangular palisaded advance work to protect the approach to the ditch, and like the Mercury Bay *pa* there is a raised stage behind the main palisade. The houses are ranged between the palisades and the flat open space (*marae*)* inside the *pa*, and at the end of the site are racks for storing fern rhizomes, and latrines. The latter were apparently a universal feature of *pa*, and are otherwise unknown in Polynesia.

The ring-ditch *pa* usually comprise roughly rectangular areas, deliberately flattened or terraced in steeper terrain, and surrounded on two or more sides by ditch and bank defences. Sometimes the defences may be doubled on weak sides, and these sites rarely exceed two hectares in size. This type has been correlated by Groube[53] with the apparent migrations recorded in the Fleet traditions from Northland to the coastal regions of Taranaki and the Bay of Plenty, where the form is common as may be seen from figure 98. It is also for this class that we have the most detailed evidence from excavations.

102

Three *pa* of ring-ditch type, at Otakanini and Waioneke on the western side of the South Kaipara Harbour, and at Kauri Point near Tauranga in the Bay of Plenty, have produced coherent sequences of construction and modification going back to the fourteenth century. Otakanini *pa*[54] covers about 1.8 hectares, and some preliminary terracing began here in the fourteenth century together with the digging of sweet potato storage pits. Around 1500 the defended area was divided into two sections – possibly an inner citadel and an outer annexe – and the inner

*The term *marae* was retained in New Zealand, as in western Polynesia, to refer to an open space in the centre of a settlement. The central Polynesian usage of the term to mean a stone temple is discussed on page 76.

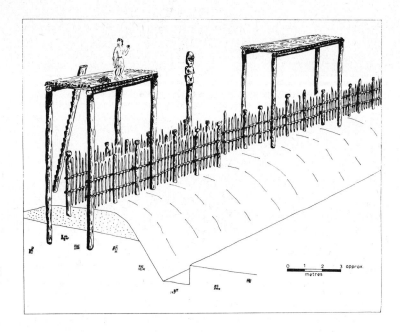

103 The fighting-stages as reconstructed from excavations at Otakanini *pa*, South Kaipara Harbour. Probably sixteenth century.

citadel in the area of the excavations was defended by a massive raised stage built on an artificial scarp, with posts sunk about two metres into the ground. Later in the sixteenth century these defences were remodelled into a ditch and inner bank with two raised stages on top. The entrance at this time was along the top of the ditch and then back along a passageway between the two rows, as described by Cook and Roux for the two sites mentioned above.

The Kauri Point *pa* had a similar pattern of development:[55] terraces and store pits from about the fourteenth century, followed at an unknown date by a ring-ditch *pa* with a double ditch on the weakest side. These ditches were later filled in with shell-midden, and, perhaps in the eighteenth century, the site was refortified over half its former area. Waioneke *pa*[56] has a similar sequence to Kauri Point, with early storage pits followed by a ring-ditch *pa*, perhaps about 1600. Like Kauri Point, the site was reduced and refortified over a small portion of its former area close to the time of European contact. These three sites suggest that simple terraced structures, presumably only weakly fortified, precede the ring-ditch structures, and the latter develop sometime in the fifteenth and sixteenth centuries. The later reduction in size of Kauri Point and Waioneke is interesting, and may reflect a pattern of increasing warfare, and the need for tightly defended citadels, in late prehistory.

Groube's hypothesis that the ring-ditch form of *pa* was spread by population movement from Northland does receive some confirmation from these excavations, although some similar dated sites from Taranaki will be needed for further support.

The earthwork types of *pa* were not the only ones constructed by the Maori, and forts built up artificially from swamps and lakes are also widely reported, especially in the Waikato region, the Hauraki Plains, and in Lake Horowhenua near Levin. Some of the Horowhenua sites were built up from standing water by piling layers of clay, gravel and rubbish within an enclosure of stakes,[57] rather like the Iron Age lake villages of Glastonbury and Meare in Somerset. Other *pa* of this type, particularly in the Waikato, were built up from swamps on the edges of lakes, normally by dumping floors of quarried sand or clay. These floors are interstratified with thick layers of occupation debris, and one site on the edge of Lake Ngaroto in the Waikato attained an eventual thickness of three metres.[58] Furthermore, the waterlogging associated with these sites has led to excellent preservation of organic materials, especially at a site on the edge of Lake Mangakaware.[59]

104 Plan of the excavated swamp *pa* by Lake Mangakaware, Waikato.

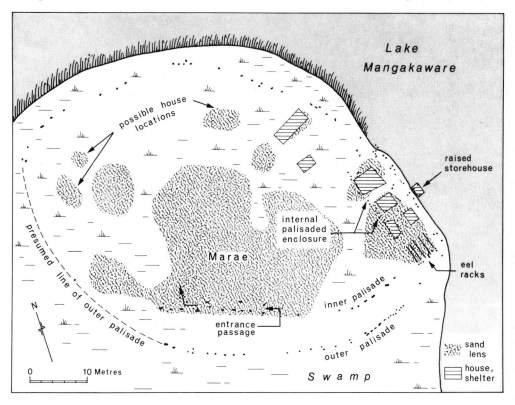

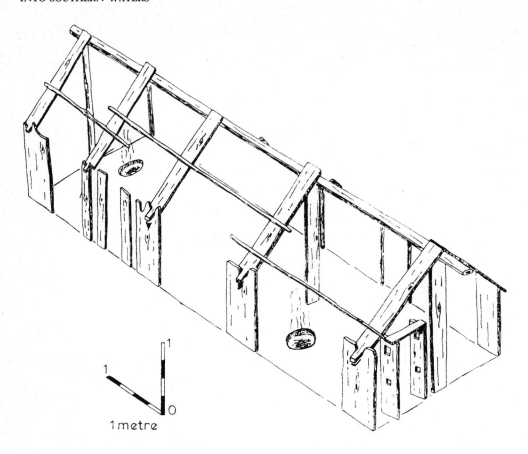

1 metre

105 Reconstructed house with partially-planked walls from the Lake Mangakaware *pa*.

The Mangakaware site covered only about 0.2 hectare, but produced excellent evidence for settlement layout, since the bases of the wooden house walls were all preserved, as were the palisades, and also many wooden artefacts thrown into the lake. Massive timber palisades driven up to three metres in the ground formed the defences, with a double row on the vulnerable landward side. The *pa* was entered through a very narrow palisaded passage similar to that reconstructed for Otakanini, and quite a number of broken weapons and ornaments were found in this passage, together with human bone and red ochre. Evidently a battle had centred on this spot, and excavations in one area inside the *pa* revealed clear traces of cannibalism.

The houses inside the site were grouped in a semicircle of six or more backing on to the lake, and facing on to an open space (*marae*) in the centre. Numerous hearths were found in this central area, but no definite structures. The largest house, 6 metres long by 2.20 wide, was built of planks and possible thatching, and its form can be reconstructed from analysis of the

many house timbers found in the lake. The other houses were 105
smaller than this one, and built either of planks or of tree-fern
posts. Economic analyses show that the site was probably settled
all year round, but by a fluctuating population, many of whom
would disperse to look after plantations in the summer, and even
to travel to the sea, 40 kilometres away, to get fish and shellfish.

Generalization is rather difficult concerning the functions of
*pa*. Some were perhaps no more than fortified hamlets occupied
on a seasonal basis, while the examples I have described above
fall into a larger category of sites perhaps occupied all year
round. Some of the largest ones situated near large harbours with
rich estuarine resources and good soils probably served as tribal
centres, with populations in the hundreds dwelling within on a
fairly permanent basis. Maximum occupation of all these sites
presumably occurred during periods of hostility, but normally it
may be assumed that each *pa* formed the node of a settlement
pattern which included coastal and seasonal shellfish middens,[60]
and small hamlets with storage pits and houses located close to
gardens.[61]

Storage pits of rectangular or bell shapes are very common in
most Classic settlements, and occurrences of these structures
have been noted several times in preceding paragraphs. The
rectangular ones are the most important, and may be up to 10
metres long, and sometimes have multiple post rows inside to
support a roof.[62] Despite a view held some years ago that such 106
pits were used as houses, it is now fairly certain that all were
originally constructed as storage pits, although many were 107
perhaps inhabited during later stages of their lives.

The field systems used for cultivation during the Classic phase
have also survived in some areas, especially on the stony volcanic
soils of Auckland and Northland where lumps of scoria were
removed and built into mounds and low linear boundary walls,
similar to the field systems in the Hawaiian Islands. Such field
systems are also known from the Archaic phase in the Wairarapa,
as noted on page 138. Agnes Sullivan has recently estimated that
perhaps 2000 hectares of the rich volcanic soil of the Auckland
Isthmus may once have supported stone boundary alignments
and mounds,[63] and an area of about 280 hectares of such
structures still survives at Wiri, on the Manukau Harbour south
of Auckland, in association with a terraced *pa* which has dated
occupation back to about AD 1300. Such field areas were
probably used for sweet potatoes and fern rhizomes in a long-
term cycle of cropping and fallow, although Maoris did

apparently have methods of increasing soil fertility by burning brushwood on fields and raking in the ash.

The New Zealand sequence, despite its span of only one thousand years, does present evidence for rather explosive cultural development in the north, of a kind unparalleled elsewhere in Polynesia. In the South Island the picture is reversed, with a gradual decrease in cultural energy owing to an unsurmountable decrease in resources. In the North Island this trend was circumvented by the development of pit storage for the essential sweet potato, and the fairly rapid rise and spread of

106 Sweet potato storage pit with drain at Taniwha *pa*, Waikato. Scale is in feet.

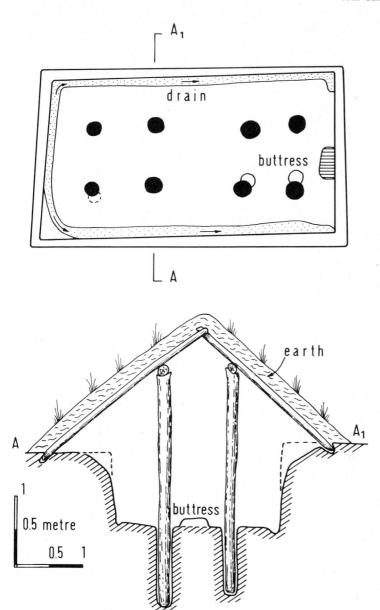

107 Roofing method for a pit like that shown in Figure 106, but with two rows of posts. The buttress is left against the wall at one end, and may have served as an access step.

Classic Maori culture gave rise to the warlike and artistic society observed by Europeans at the end of the eighteenth century. The eventual introduction of muskets, metal tools, new crops, pigs, whaleboats and a new religion wrought massive changes in Maori society by 1840, but the Polynesian origins of the Maori people have remained clear, even in the increasingly westernized New Zealand society of today.

# 6

# The achievements of the Polynesians

Prehistoric research in Polynesia since the Second World War has established some very basic facts which few people would now challenge lightly. The Polynesians are speakers of Austronesian languages, and they belong to the Mongoloid group of mankind, albeit with some Melanesian genetic admixture. Their origins can be traced to the eastern islands of South-East Asia in the second millennium BC, whence they moved, mainly through Melanesia, into the western islands of Polynesia by about 1500–1000 BC. Some movement through Micronesia has also been postulated by other authors, but this is difficult to verify at present. Once established in western Polynesia the Polynesians began to expand further – on into eastern Polynesia, which was settled mainly between AD 1 and 1000, and back into the region of the Polynesian outliers. The time span of 2000 years required to settle all points of the Polynesian triangle may seem long, but as pointed out in the introduction this was the largest region in the world ever to be settled by a single ethnic group. Apart from possible drifts from America, or perhaps even Japan, we have no indications that any people but the Polynesians ever settled in the triangle.

The first settlers of western Polynesia belonged to the Lapita Culture (c. 1300–500 BC) as defined by archaeological research; they may be described as horticulturists, coastal fishermen, and makers of pottery and ground-stone tools. They perhaps lived in fairly large sedentary villages, and they certainly had a well-developed knowledge of canoe construction and ocean navigation. Views on Polynesian navigational ability have swung from negative to positive several times over the past 200 years, and I do not wish to become embroiled in a rather specialized debate. However, the 2000-year time-span of settlement makes it unlikely that exploring expeditions were sent out with any great regularity, and the Polynesians were certainly not foolhardy in the undertaking and planning of a voyage. They doubtless knew from Lapita days that long-distance exploring canoes rarely came home, and it seems to me that the fully-stocked double canoes so beloved of anthropologists would only set out at times of insecurity, warfare, famine, or some other dire pressure on resources. Such situations do not of course develop overnight, and after one island was settled it may have been many years before any of its inhabitants felt constrained to give up all and cast themselves on the mercy of Tangaroa. Perhaps the greater number of these voyagers drowned in unknown waters, and we shall never know what the actual loss-rate was in the discovery of a locality such as Easter Island. On the other hand, only ten successful voyages of over 1000 kilometres would probably account for the settlement of the whole Polynesian triangle.

Economically, the Polynesians not only settled small islands lacking in useful terrestrial resources, but they also introduced a range of domesticated crops and animals, and developed systems of slash-and-burn and irrigation horticulture which excited the admiration of many early European visitors. The missionary John Williams described the appearance of the Rarotongan coastal strip in 1823 as follows:

> In the first place there are rows of superb chestnut trees, *inocarpus*, planted at equal distances, and stretching from the mountain's base to the sea, with a space between each row of about half-a-mile wide. This space is divided into small *taro* beds, which are dug four feet deep, and can be irrigated at pleasure. These average about half an acre each. The embankments around each bed are thrown up with a slope, leaving a flat surface on the top of six or eight feet in width. The lowest parts are planted with *taro*, and the sides of the embankment with *kape* or gigantic *taro*, while on the top are placed, at regular intervals, small beautifully shaped bread-fruit trees.[1]

Such a regular layout, together with the amount of labour obviously required, suggests a very high degree of co-operation among the members of the society. In Polynesia, the aristocratic patterns of ranking undoubtedly provided the major channels through which such co-operation could operate, and it would be of some interest to know how these aspects of Polynesian social structure developed. Because they are found so widely it is unlikely that they have developed independently, and they must surely have been present in the original society of the Lapita settlers. Chiefdoms with genealogical ranking supported by religious sanctions are of course found widely throughout the world, but in the western Pacific they are rather rare, indeed absent in most parts of Island South-East Asia (excluding the regions affected by Indianization) and Melanesia.

This is, in fact, rather an interesting circumstance. Because there are no peoples in Island South-East Asia, with the possible exception of Taiwan, who have ranked chiefdoms on the Polynesian pattern, we clearly cannot point out any possible Polynesian homeland on these criteria. But it may be that the Polynesians and their ancestors were the only groups to develop such systems – perhaps these are what provided the impetus and organization to settle Polynesia in the first place. Perhaps we can extend this argument further and suggest that the Lapita process of expansion itself, with establishment of settlements and exchange networks among unrelated and perhaps hostile Melanesian peoples, provided the impetus for increasing social integration. If the early Lapita societies had headmen or 'Big Men' with higher than average prestige, then it is perhaps not hard to see how the rigours of expansion provided a long-term and continuous stimulus to maintain a central authority and social cohesion. Sons might then succeed their prestigious fathers, and religion, often embellished in periods of social change and stress, could be called upon to validate an eventual pattern of hereditary aristocracy. Naturally, I can hardly prove this view in any conclusive fashion, but the period of Lapita expansion surely was an extraordinary one in the life-history of the Austronesians, and it was also a very successful one.

The later stages in the development of Polynesian chiefdoms have been described especially in Chapter 4. Once the large and fertile islands such as Tahiti, the Hawaiian Islands, Samoa and Tonga were settled, then the growth of large, dense populations clearly gave added support to the process. Of course, no Polynesian society ever developed a unified and state-like system of organization, partly because the islands were too small and isolated, and also because no single chief was ever able to dominate his competitors in any enduring fashion. The reasons for this may lie partly in the relatively undeveloped methods of warfare and transport, for it is clear that the Hawaiian, Tongan and Society Islands were very quickly unified by force once European ideas and arms entered the arena. Whether unified states would eventually have evolved in some of the Polynesian groups without outside influence is a question which can hardly be answered.

The over-all shape of the Polynesian achievement prior to AD 1800 has been the central theme of this book, and I have tried to summarize a few of the main points in this final short chapter. On a world scale the Polynesians clearly achieved a great deal, especially when we consider their isolation from major continental centres of cultural development, and their neolithic technology. But there is one other observation about Polynesia which should be of particular interest to prehistorians and anthropologists. This concerns the nature and visibility of adaptation.

The Polynesians, as we now know, are of unified origin; their languages, physical type and social customs indicate this quite clearly. The adaptations which we can observe have all developed within the past three thousand years from a single base-line society whose characteristics can be partially reconstructed, and they have also developed without any major outside influence. This means that the role of environment can be seen in a particularly clear light. The Maoris of temperate New Zealand, the people of sub-tropical Easter Island, the atoll dwellers, the highly ranked societies of lush tropical Tahiti and Hawaii, and the forgotten visitors to Pitcairn and Necker all developed rather different societies (or mysteries) to greet the first European visitors. Each received the distinctive stamp of its environmental milieu, and while Polynesian societies could not compete with those of Melanesia in terms of linguistic, social or racial diversity, they provided fair competition in the fields of economy and political organization. This is one reason why economic prehistory has become so important in recent years, particularly in New Zealand and Hawaii. Environments clearly were of outstanding importance.

At the time of writing, prehistoric research in Polynesia is going through a fairly quiet phase, except in the highly westernized societies of Hawaii and New Zealand. More resources are being concentrated in Melanesia and South-East Asia, and this is perhaps as it should be. These areas do hold the clues to the ultimate origins of the Polynesians, and as research progresses we should know more of how the Polynesians relate to the people who are, after all, their closest extra-Oceanic relatives: the Indonesians, the Filipinos, and even the Chinese, Thais and Vietnamese of the mainland of South-East Asia.

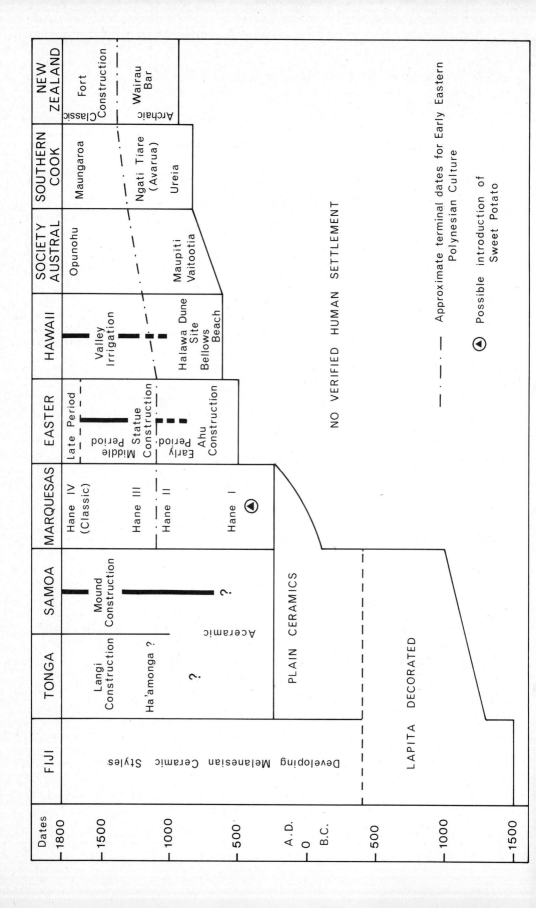

# Notes

## Chapter 1

1 On Pacific island geography see Thomas 1967. Polynesia has a total of 287 islands (listed in Douglas 1969).
2 A list of recorded drift voyages is given in Golson 1973.
3 Levison, Ward and Webb 1973.
4 For general surveys see Sharp 1960; Washburn 1967.
5 For the journals of Cook and Banks see Beaglehole in the bibliography.
6 Sterndale 1874:20.
7 For a general survey of earlier theories see Howard 1967.
8 Hale 1846.
9 Smith 1898-9.
10 Handy 1930a; 1930b.
11 Piddington 1939.
12 Buck 1944, and see also Buck 1938.
13 Heyerdahl 1950.
14 Heyerdahl 1952.
15 Burrows 1938.
16 The Polynesian Outliers are as follows: Nukuoro and Kapingamarangi (Caroline Islands); Nukuria, Takuu, Nukumanu, Luangiua (Ontong Java), Sikaiana, Rennell and Bellona (Solomon Islands); Pileni and Taumako (Santa Cruz Islands); Tikopia and Anuta (eastern Solomons); Mae, Aniwa, Futuna, Mele and Fila (New Hebrides), Uvea (Loyalty Islands).

## Chapter 2

1 The term Australoid is here used to cover the Melanesians as well as the aborigines of Australia. See Coon 1966; Bellwood 1975.
2 For a general survey of Polynesian physical anthropology see Howells 1973.
3 Simmons 1962.
4 Langdon 1975.
5 Pietrusewsky 1970.
6 For a general survey of Austronesian languages see Pawley 1974.
7 Pawley and Green 1975; Blust 1976.
8 Compiled from Green 1966; Pawley 1966.

9 The Eastern Oceanic subgroup is described in Pawley 1972.
10 See Pawley 1967 on outlier languages.
11 For a list see Walsh and Biggs 1966.
12 Firth 1957.
13 The situation in the Tokelaus is described by Hooper (1968).
14 Goldman 1970.
15 Sahlins 1958.
16 On early plant domestication in the Pacific see Barrau 1965; Bellwood 1976; Yen 1973.
17 For example Sauer 1952; Solheim 1970.
18 For a very full account of the sweet potato see Yen 1974.
19 For reports on these excavations see Ladd and Yen 1972; Kirch and Kelly 1975.
20 On canoes see Haddon and Hornell 1936-8. For a general account of Polynesian navigation see Lewis 1972.
21 Corney 1913-9, vol II:285-6.
22 The extent of this knowledge is described by Lewthwaite (1967).
23 Sharp 1963 (published as an earlier version in Sharp 1956).
24 Described in Gladwin 1970; Lewis 1972.
25 See Lewis 1976 for a popular account.

## Chapter 3

1 For a full survey see Bellwood 1977a.
2 Recent work by Professor Jack Golson, Australian National University, at the Kuk plantation near Mt. Hagen. For published report on this site see Golson 1977.
3 Solheim 1968.
4 See Bellwood 1977a, Chapter 9.
5 See Mead et al. 1973 and Green 1976a for discussions of Lapita decoration.
6 Sites of this size are reported by Green (1976b) in the Santa Cruz Islands.
7 Ambrose and Green 1972. The Lapita people also used obsidian from the Admiralty Islands (north of New Guinea) and Tonga.
8 Howells 1973.
9 Shutler and Marck 1975.
10 Dyen 1965 – Polynesian and Indonesian languages

are placed together in his Malayo–Polynesian linkage.

11 This is discussed by Davidson (1976).

12 The Tongan sites are described in Poulsen 1967, Groube 1971.

13 Green and Davidson 1969; 1974: Jennings 1976.

14 The culture history of the outliers is discussed by Bayard (1966) and Davidson (1970; 1974).

15 For Futuna see Kirch 1976; for Bellona see Poulsen 1972; and for Anuta see Kirch and Rosendahl 1973.

16 Bellwood 1977a, chapter 11.

17 Sinoto 1970; see also Bellwood 1970.

18 Dickinson and Shutler 1974.

19 Sinoto 1966; 1970.

20 Kirch 1973.

21 Sinoto and McCoy 1975.

22 See Kirch 1974 for a general discussion of early Hawaiian sites.

23 Morgenstein and Riley 1974.

24 Ayres 1971.

25 Duff 1956; Trotter 1974.

## Chapter 4

1 For details see Goldman 1970. Tongan society at the beginning of the nineteenth century is described in Mariner 1817, and the basic ethnographic account is Gifford 1929.

2 Described in McKern 1929; Davidson 1971.

3 Davidson 1969a.

4 Good general accounts of Samoan society may be found in Mead 1969, Gilson 1970 and Freeman 1964.

5 Samoan settlement patterns are discussed by Davidson 1969b, and by Green 1970.

6 For a general account of *marae* architecture see Emory 1970.

7 Green 1971.

8 Duff 1956, 1959.

9 As documented by Buck (1944).

10 Oliver 1974. See also Goldman 1970.

11 Emory 1933. See also Green and Green 1968.

12 Green *et al.* 1967; Green 1961.

13 Emory 1934, 1970.

14 Emory 1939.

15 Emory (1947) gives a good account of *marae* function in the Tuamotus.

16 Verin 1969.

17 Heyerdahl and Ferdon 1965, reports 2–4.

18 For a general account of the Cooks see Buck 1944. Recent archaeological work is described in Trotter (ed.) 1974; Bellwood 1977b.

19 Cook Island *marae* are described in Bellwood 1969.

20 See Bellwood 1974.

21 Described in Bellwood 1977b.

22 See Bellwood 1971a.

23 Sinoto 1970.

24 See especially Suggs 1961; Kellum-Ottino 1971; Bellwood 1972.

25 Suggs 1960: 124.

26 See Heyerdahl and Ferdon 1965: 117–51.

27 Dening (ed.) 1974: 181.

28 Schmitt 1971.

29 Emory 1959; Cordy 1974.

30 Goldman 1970: 212.

31 Summers 1964; Kikuchi 1976.

32 Emory 1928.

33 On Hawaiian images see Cox and Davenport 1974.

34 Ellis 1969: 164; Ladd 1969.

35 Green (ed.) 1969; 1970: Ladd and Yen 1972; Ladd 1973.

36 Kirch and Kelly 1975.

37 Newman 1970: Tuggle and Griffin 1973.

38 Cox 1970.

39 For a summary of research on Pitcairn see Heyerdahl and Skjölsvold, 1965.

## Chapter 5

1 Full reports of the Norwegian expedition can be found in Heyerdahl and Ferdon (eds.) 1961 (reviewed in detail by Golson 1965), and in Heyerdahl 1976; see also Heyerdahl 1968.

2 See especially Mulloy's reports in the Bulletin series of the Easter Island Committee, International Fund for Monuments Inc; Ayres 1971; McCoy, 1973.

3 McCoy 1971.

4 Apart from the journals of the explorers mentioned in the text, good general accounts of Easter Island will be found in Routledge 1919; Métraux 1940; Englert 1970. Métraux is the major source for ethnography.

5 Summarized very concisely in Smith 1962.

6 Mulloy 1961.

7 Ayres 1971.

8 For descriptions of the statues and quarries see Routledge 1919; Skjölsvold 1961.

9 Mulloy 1970.

10 The Orongo village is described by Routledge 1920, Ferdon 1961; Mulloy 1975.

11 See Heyerdahl 1958, in addition to the works mentioned in footnote 1.

12 Brand 1971.

13 Golson 1965.

14 Lanning 1970.

15 Barthel 1971.

16 Métraux 1940: 399–405.

17 Emory 1972.

18 For Polynesian adaptations to New Zealand see Green 1974.

19 On moas see Simmons 1968.

20 K. Shawcross 1967.

21 For a recent estimate of New Zealand's prehistoric population see Shawcross 1970.

22 Green 1967; Sinoto 1968.

23 See Duff 1956.

24 Golson 1959.

25 Skinner 1974: 76–82.

26 Leach 1969.

27 See, for example, Wilkes and Scarlett 1967.

28 e.g. Leahy 1976 for the Taupo region.

29 Shawcross 1972; 1975.

30 e.g. by Duff 1956.

31 Groube 1968: 143; H. Leach 1974.

32 Davidson 1975.

33 Park 1970; Yen 1961.

34 H. Leach 1974.
35 Simmons 1973.
36 See Cumberland 1962.
37 Trotter and McCulloch 1971; Ambrose 1970.
38 Richards 1972. See also Skinner 1923; Skinner and Baucke 1928 on Moriori ethnography.
39 This assemblage is described most fully in Golson 1959.
40 e.g. by Duff 1956.
41 Shawcross 1964.
42 Adkin 1948 (Horowhenua); Bellwood in press (Mangakaware).
43 Groube 1970.
44 Sharp 1956b.
45 Groube 1970.
46 Simmons 1969.
47 Mead 1975.
48 Hamilton 1896; Barrow 1969.
49 Groube 1970. General descriptions of *pa* may be found in Best 1927; Fox 1976.

50 Comparisons with British hillforts are made by Fox 1976.
51 Reed 1969: 61–2; Beaglehole 1962, part I: 433.
52 See Kelly 1951.
53 Groube 1970.
54 Bellwood 1971b.
55 Golson 1961; Ambrose 1962 and personal communication.
56 McKinlay 1971.
57 Adkin 1948.
58 Shawcross 1968.
59 Bellwood in press.
60 See the example described by Shawcross 1967.
61 e.g. Davidson 1972.
62 Fox 1974.
63 Sullivan 1974.

## Chapter 6

1 Williams 1838: 206–7.

# Bibliography

## Abbreviations

| | |
|---|---|
| *APAO* | Archaeology and Physical Anthropology in Oceania |
| *BPBMB* | Bernice P. Bishop Museum Bulletin |
| *BPBMM* | Bernice P. Bishop Museum Memoir |
| *BPBMOP* | Bernice P. Bishop Museum Occasional Paper |
| *BPBMSP* | Bernice P. Bishop Museum Special Publication |
| *JPS* | Journal of the Polynesian Society |
| *JSO* | Journal de la Société des Océanistes |
| *NZAAN* | New Zealand Archaeological Association Newsletter |
| *PAR* | Pacific Anthropological Records |
| *PPS* | Proceedings of the Prehistoric Society |
| *RAIM* | Records of the Auckland Institute and Museum |

ADKIN, G. L. 1948. *Horowhenua*. Wellington: Polynesian Society Memoir 26.

AMBROSE, W. 1963. Further investigations at Kauri Point. *NZAAN* 5: 56–66.

— 1970. Archaeology and rock-drawings from the Waitaki Gorge, Central South Island. *Records of the Canterbury Museum* 8: 383–437.

AMBROSE, W. and R. C. GREEN 1972. First millennium B C transport of obsidian from New Britain to the Solomon Islands. *Nature* 237: 31.

AYRES, W. 1971. Radiocarbon dates from Easter Island. *JPS* 80: 497–504.

BARRAU, J. 1965. Histoire et préhistoire horticoles de l'Océanie tropicale. *JSO* 21: 55–78.

BARROW, T. 1969. *Maori wood sculpture of New Zealand*. Wellington: Reed.

BARTHEL, T. 1971. Pre-contact writing in Oceania, *in* Seboek T. (ed.) *Linguistics in Oceania*, p. 1165–1168. The Hague: Mouton.

BAYARD, D. T. 1966. *The cultural relationships of the Polynesian outliers*. Unpublished M.A. thesis, University of Hawaii.

BEAGLEHOLE, J. C. (ed.) 1962. *The Endeavour Journal of Joseph Banks 1768–1771*. 2 vols. Sydney: Trustees of the Public Library of New South Wales.

— 1967–9. *The Journals of Captain James Cook on his voyage of discovery*. 5 vols. Cambridge: Hakluyt Society.

BELLWOOD, P. S. 1969. Archaeology on Rarotonga and Aitutaki, Cook Islands. *JPS* 78: 517–30.

— 1970. Dispersal centres in East Polynesia, with special reference to the Society and Marquesas Islands, *in* Green, R. C. and M. Kelly (eds.) 1970: 93–104.

— 1971a. Varieties of ecological adaptation in the southern Cook Islands. *APAO* 6: 145–69.

— 1971b. Fortifications and economy in prehistoric New Zealand. *PPS* 37: 56–95

— 1972. *A settlement pattern survey, Hanatekua Valley, Hiva Oa, Marquesas Islands*. *PAR* 17.

— 1974. Prehistoric contacts in the Cook Islands. *Mankind* 9: 278–80.

— 1975. The prehistory of Oceania. *Current Anthropology*, 16: 9–28.

— 1976. Prehistoric plant and animal domestication in Austronesia, *in* Sieveking G. *et al.* (eds.), *Problems in economic and social archaeology*, p. 153–68. London: Duckworth.

— 1977a. *Man's Conquest of the Pacific*. London: Collins.

— 1977b. *Archaeological research in the Cook Islands*. *PAR* forthcoming.

— in press. *Archaeological research at Lake Mangakaware, Waikato 1968–70*. NZAA Monograph, forthcoming.

BEST, E. 1927. *The Pa Maori*. Wellington: Dominion Museum Bulletin 6.

BLUST, R. A. 1976. Austronesian culture history: some linguistic inferences and their relations to the archaeological record. *World Archaeology* 8: 19–43.

BRAND, D. B. 1971. The sweet potato: an exercise in methodology, *in* Riley, C. L. *et al.* (eds.), *Man across the sea*, p. 343–65. Austin and London: University of Texas Press.

BUCK, Sir Peter 1938. *Vikings of the Sunrise*. New York: Stokes.

— 1944. *Arts and crafts of the Cook Islands*. *BPBMB* 179.

BURROWS, E. G. 1938. *Western Polynesia: a study of cultural differentiation*. Göteborg: Ethnologiska Studier 7.

COON, C. S. 1966. *The living races of man*. London: Jonathan Cape.

CORDY, R. H. 1974. Cultural adaptation and evolution in Hawaii: a suggested new sequence. *JPS* 83: 180–91.

CORNEY, B. G. (ed.) 1913–19. *The quest and occupation of Tahiti by emissaries of Spain during the years 1772–6*. 3 volumes. Hakluyt Society.

Cox, J. H. 1970. *Hawaiian petroglyphs. BPBMSP* 60.

Cox, J. H. and W. Davenport 1974. *Hawaiian sculpture.* Honolulu, University of Hawaii Press.

Cumberland, K. B. 1962. Moas and men: New Zealand about A.D. 1250. *Geographical Review* 52: 151–73.

Davidson, J. M. 1969a. Archaeological excavations in two burial mounds at 'Atele, Tongatapu. *RAIM* 6: 251–86.

—1969b. Settlement patterns in Samoa before 1840. *JPS* 78: 44–82.

—1970. Polynesian outliers and the problem of culture replacement in small populations, *in* Green R. C. and M. Kelly (eds.) 1970: 61–72.

—1971. Preliminary report on an archaeological survey of the Vava'u Group, Tonga, *in Cook Bicentenary Expedition in the South-west Pacific* p. 29–40. Royal Society of New Zealand Bulletin 8.

—1972. Archaeological excavations on Motutapu Island, New Zealand. *RAIM* 9: 1–14.

—1974. Cultural replacements on small islands: new evidence from Polynesian outliers. *Mankind* 9: 273–7.

—1975. The excavation of Skipper's Ridge (N40/7), Opito, Coromandel Peninsula, in 1959 and 1960. *RAIM* 12: 1–42.

—1976. The prehistory of western Polynesia, *in IX^e Congrès Union Internationale des Sciences Préhistoriques et Protohistoriques*, colloque XXII, p. 27–51. Paris: Centre National de la Recherche Scientifique.

Dening, G. M. 1974. *The Marquesan journal of Edward Robarts, 1797–1824.* Canberra: Australian National University Press.

Dickinson W. R. and R. Shutler 1974. Probable Fijian origin of quartzose temper sands in prehistoric pottery from Tonga and the Marquesas Islands. *Science* 185: 454–7.

Douglas, G. 1969. Check list of Pacific Oceanic islands. *Micronesica* 5: 327–464.

Duff, R. 1956. *The moa-hunter period of Maori culture.* 2nd edition. Wellington: Government Printer.

—1959. Neolithic adzes of eastern Polynesia, *in* Freeman J. D. and W. R. Geddes (eds.) *Anthropology in the South Seas*, p. 121–48. New Plymouth: Avery.

Dyen, I. 1965. *A lexicostatistical classification of the Austronesian languages.* International Journal of American Linguistics, Memoir 19.

Ellis, W. 1969. *Polynesian researches: Hawaii.* 1842 edition reissued by Charles E. Tuttle.

Emory, K. P. 1928. *Archaeology of Nihoa and Necker Islands. BPBMB* 53.

—1933. *Stone remains in the Society Islands. BPBMB* 116.

—1934. *Tuamotuan stone structures. BPBMB* 118.

—1939. *Archaeology of Mangareva and neighbouring atolls. BPBMB* 163.

—1947. *Tuamotuan religious structures and ceremonies. BPBMB* 191.

—1959. Origin of the Hawaiians. *JPS* 68: 29–35.

—1970. A re-examination of East-Polynesian marae: many marae later, *in* Green, R. C. and M. Kelly (eds.) 1970: 73–92.

—1972. Easter Island's position in the prehistory of Polynesia. *JPS* 81: 57–69.

Englert, S. 1970. *Island at the centre of the world.* London: Hale.

Ferdon, E. N. 1961. The ceremonial site of Orongo, *in* Heyerdahl T. and E. N. Ferdon (eds.) 1961: 221–56.

Firth, R. 1957. A note on descent groups in Polynesia. *Man* 57: 4–8.

Fox, A. 1974. Prehistoric Maori storage pits: problems in interpretation. *JPS* 83: 141–54.

—1976. *Prehistoric Maori fortifications.* Auckland: Longman Paul.

Freeman, J. D. 1964. Some observations on kinship and political structure in Samoa. *American Anthropologist* 66: 553–68.

Gifford, E. W. 1929. *Tongan Society. BPBMB* 61.

Gilson, R. P. 1970. *Samoa 1830 to 1900.* Melbourne: Oxford University Press.

Gladwin, T. 1970. *East is a big bird.* Harvard University Press.

Goldman, I. 1970. *Ancient Polynesian Society.* University of Chicago Press.

Golson, J. 1959. Culture change in prehistoric New Zealand, *in* Freeman, J. D. and W. R. Geddes (eds.) *Anthropology in the South Seas*, p. 29–74, New Plymouth: Avery.

—1961. Investigations at Kauri Point, Katikati. *NZAAN* 4: 13–41.

—1965. Thor Heyerdahl and the prehistory of Easter Island. *Oceania* 36: 38–83.

—(ed.) 1973. *Polynesian navigation.* Wellington: Polynesian Society Memoir 34.

—1977. No room at the top: agricultural intensification in the New Guinea Highlands, *in* Allen J. *et al.* (eds.) *Sunda and Sahul*, p. 601–38. London: Academic Press.

Green, R. C. 1961. Moorean archaeology: a preliminary report. *Man* 61: 169–73.

—1966. Linguistic subgrouping within Polynesia. *JPS* 75: 3–35.

—1967. Sources of New Zealand's East Polynesian culture: the evidence of a pearl-shell lure shank. *APAO* 2: 81–90.

—(ed.) 1969. *Makaha Valley Historical Project: interim report 1.PAR* 4.

—1970. Settlement pattern archaeology in Polynesia, *in* Green, R. C. and M. Kelly (eds.) 1970: 13–32.

—1971. Evidence for the development of the early Polynesian adze kit. *NZAAN* 14: 12–44.

—1974. Adaptation and change in Maori culture, *in* Kuschel G. (ed.), *Ecology and biogeography in New Zealand*, p. 1–44. The Hague: Junk.

—1976a. New sites with Lapita pottery and their implications for an understanding of the settlement of the western Pacific, *in IX^e Congrés Union Internationale des Sciences Préhistoriques et Protohistoriques*, Colloque XXII, p. 55–87. Paris: Centre National de la Recherche Scientifique.

—1976b. Lapita sites in the Santa Cruz group, *in* Green R. C. and M. M. Cresswell (eds.) *Southeast Solomon Islands culture history*, p. 245–65. Royal Society of New Zealand Bulletin 11.

GREEN, R. C. and J. M. DAVIDSON (eds.) 1969. *Archaeology in Western Samoa*. Volume 1. Bulletin of the Auckland Institute and Museum 6.

—1974. *Archaeology in Western Samoa*. Volume 2. Bulletin of the Auckland Institute and Museum 7.

GREEN R. C. and K. GREEN, 1968. Religious structures (marae) of the Windward Society Islands. *NZ Journal of History* 2: 66–89.

GREEN, R. C., K. GREEN, R. A. RAPPAPORT, A. RAPPAPORT and J. M. DAVIDSON 1967. *Archaeology on the Island of Mo'orea, French Polynesia*. Anthropological papers of the American Museum of Natural History 51, part 2.

GREEN, R. C. and M. KELLY (eds.) 1970. *Studies in Oceanic culture history*. Volume 1. *PAR* 11.

—1971. *Studies in Oceanic culture history*. Volume 2. *PAR* 12.

GROUBE, L. M. 1968. Research in New Zealand prehistory since 1956 *in* Yawata I. and Y. H. Sinoto (eds.) *Prehistoric culture in Oceania*, p. 141–9. Honolulu: Bishop Museum Press.

—1970. The origin and development of earthwork fortification in the Pacific, *in* Green R. C. and M. Kelly (eds.) 1970: 133–64.

—1971. Tonga, Lapita pottery, and Polynesian origins. *JPS* 80: 278–316.

HADDON, A. C. and J. HORNELL 1936–8. *The canoes of Oceania*. 3 volumes, *BPBMSP* 27, 28 and 29.

HALE, H. 1846. *United States Exploring Expedition 1838–42: ethnography and philology*. Philadelphia: Lea and Blanchard.

HAMILTON, A. 1896. *The art workmanship of the Maori race in New Zealand*. Wellington: New Zealand Institute.

HANDY, E. S. C. 1930a. *The problem of Polynesian origins. BPBMOP* 9 part 8.

—1930b. *History and culture in the Society Islands. BPBMB* 79.

HEYERDAHL, T. 1950. *The Kon-Tiki Expedition*. London: Allen and Unwin.

—1952. *American Indians in the Pacific*. London, Allen and Unwin.

—1958. *Aku-Aku*. London: Allen and Unwin.

—1968. *Sea routes to Polynesia*. London: Allen and Unwin.

—1976. *The art of Easter Island*. London: Allen and Unwin.

HEYERDAHL, T. and E. N. FERDON (eds.) 1961. *Reports of the Norwegian Archaeological Expedition to Easter Island and the East Pacific, volume 1: archaeology of Easter Island*. School of American Research and Museum of New Mexico. Monograph 24, part 1, Santa Fe, New Mexico.

—1965. *Reports of the Norwegian Archaeological Expedition to Easter Island and the East Pacific, volume 2: miscellaneous papers*. School of American Research and Kon-Tiki Museum, Monograph 24, part 2, Stockholm.

HEYERDAHL, T. and A. SKJÖLSVOLD 1965. Notes on the archaeology of Pitcairn, *in* Heyerdahl T. and E. N. Ferdon (eds.) 1965: 3–8.

HOOPER, A. 1968. Socio-economic organisation of the Tokelau Islands. *8th Congress of Anthropological and Ethnological Sciences*, vol. 2: 238–40. Tokyo and Kyoto.

HOWARD, A. 1967. Polynesian origins and migrations: a review of two centuries of speculation and theory, *in* Highland G. *et al.* (eds.) *Polynesian culture history*. p. 45–102. *BPBMSP* 56.

HOWELLS, W. W. 1973. *The Pacific Islanders*. New York: Scribner's Sons.

JENNINGS, J. D. (ed.) 1976. *Excavations on Upolu, Western Samoa. PAR* 25.

KELLUM-OTTINO, M. 1971. *Archéologie d'une vallée des Îles Marquises*. Paris: Publication de la Société des Océanistes 26.

KELLY, L. G. 1951. *Marion du Fresne at the Bay of Islands*. Wellington: Reed.

KIKUCHI, W. K. 1976. Prehistoric Hawaiian fishponds. *Science* 193: 295–9.

KIRCH, P. V. 1973. Prehistoric subsistence patterns in the northern Marquesas Islands, French Polynesia. *APAO* 8: 24–40.

—1974. The chronology of early Hawaiian settlement. *APAO* 9: 110–9.

—1976. Ethno-archaeological investigations in Futuna and Uvea (western Polynesia): a preliminary report. *JPS* 85: 27–70.

KIRCH, P. V. and M. KELLY (eds.) 1975. *Prehistory and ecology in a windward Hawaiian Valley: Halawa Valley, Molokai. PAR* 24.

KIRCH, P. V. and P. H. ROSENDAHL 1973. Archaeological investigation of Anuta, *in* Yen D. E. and J. Gordon (eds.), *Anuta: a Polynesian outlier in the Solomon Islands*, p. 25–108, *PAR* 21.

LADD. E. J. 1969. Hale-o-Keawe temple site, Honaunau: pre-salvage report. *Asian and Pacific Archaeology Series* 3: 163–90.

LADD, E. J. (ed.) 1973. *Makaha Valley Historical Project: interim report 4. PAR* 19.

LADD, E. J. and D. YEN 1972. *Makaha Valley Historical Project: Interim report 3 PAR* 18.

LANGDON, R. 1975. *The lost caravel*. Sydney: Pacific Publications.

LANNING, E. P. 1971. South America as a source for aspects of Oceanic cultures, *in* Green, R. C. and M. Kelly (eds.) 1970: 175–82.

LEACH, B. F. 1976. *The concept of similarity in prehistoric studies*. Otago University, Studies in Prehistoric Anthropology Volume 1.

LEACH, H. 1974. Pre-European. *New Zealand's Nature Heritage* 1: 117–22.

LEAHY, A. 1976. Whakamoenga Cave, Taupo, N94/7. *RAIM* 13: 29–75.

LEVISON, M., R. G. WARD and J. W. WEBB 1973. *The settlement of Polynesia: a computer simulation*. Minneapolis: University of Minnesota Press.

LEWIS, D. 1972. *We, the navigators*. Canberra: Australian National University Press.

—1976. 'Hokule'a' follows the stars to Tahiti.

*National Geographic Magazine* 150, no. 4: 513–37.

LEWTHWAITE, G. R. 1967. The geographical knowledge of the Pacific peoples, *in* Friis H. R. (ed.), *The Pacific Basin*, p. 57–86. New York: American Geographical Society.

McCoy, P. C. 1971. Review of Englert S. 1970. *JPS* 80: 259–60.

—1973. Excavation of a rectangular house on the east rim of Rano Kau volcano, Easter Island. *APAO* 8: 51–67.

McKern, W. C. 1929. *Archaeology of Tonga. BPBMB* 60.

McKinlay, J. R. 1971. Waioneke 1968–9. *NZAAN* 14: 86–9.

Mariner, W. 1817. *An account of the natives of the Tonga Islands*. London.

Mead, M. 1969. *Social organisation of Manu'a*. New York: Krauss. First published as *BPBMB* 76, 1930.

Mead, S. M. 1975. The origins of Maori art: Polynesian or Chinese? *Oceania* 45: 173–211.

Mead, S. M., L. Birks, H. Birks and E. Shaw 1973. *The Lapita pottery style of Fiji and its associations*. Polynesian Society memoir 38.

Métraux, A. 1940. *Ethnology of Easter Island. BPBMB* 160.

Morgenstein, M. and T. J. Riley 1974. Hydration-rind dating of basaltic glass: a new method for archaeological chronologies. *Asian Perspectives* 17: 145–59.

Mulloy, W. 1961. The ceremonial centre of Vinapu, *in* Heyerdahl, T. and E. N. Ferdon (eds.) 1961: 93–180.

—1970. A speculative reconstruction of techniques of carving, transporting and erecting Easter Island statues. *APAO* 5: 1–23.

—1975. *Investigation and restoration of the ceremonial centre of Orongo, Easter Island, part 1*. Easter Island Committee, International Fund for Monuments Inc., Bulletin, 4.

Newman, T. S. 1970. *Hawaiian fishing and farming on the island of Hawaii in AD 1788*. Honolulu: Division of State Parks.

Oliver, D. L. 1974. *Ancient Tahitian Society*. 3 vols. Honolulu: University of Hawaii Press.

Park, G. N. 1970. Palaeoclimatic change in the last 1000 years. *Tuatara* 18: 114–23.

Pawley, A. K. 1966. Polynesian languages: a subgrouping based on shared innovations in morphology. *JPS* 75: 37–62.

—1967. The relationships of Polynesian outlier languages. *JPS* 76: 259–96.

—1972. On the internal relationships of Eastern Oceanic languages. *PAR* 13: 1–142.

—1974. Austronesian languages. *Encyclopaedia Britannica (15th edition), Macropaedia* 2: 484–94.

Pawley, A. K. and R. C. Green 1975. Dating the dispersal of the Oceanic languages. *Oceanic Linguistics* 12 (1): 1–67.

Piddington, R. O. 1939. *Essays in Polynesian ethnology*. Cambridge University Press.

Pietrusewsky, M. 1970. An osteological view of indigenous populations in Polynesia, *in* Green, R. C. and M. Kelly (eds.) 1970: 1–12.

Poulsen, J. 1967. *A contribution to the prehistory of the Tongan Islands*. Unpublished Ph.D thesis, Australian National University.

—1972. Outlier prehistory: Bellona. *APAO* 7: 184–205.

Reed, A. H. and A. W. 1969. *Captain Cook in New Zealand*. Wellington: Reed.

Richards, R. 1972. A population distribution map of the Morioris of the Chatham Islands, *circa* 1790. *JPS* 81: 350–74.

Routledge, C. S. 1919. *The mystery of Easter Island*. 2nd edition. London: Sifton Praed.

—1920. Survey of the village and carved rocks of Orongo, Easter Island, by the Mana Expedition. *Journal of the Anthropological Institute* 50: 425–51.

Sahlins, M. D. 1958. *Social stratification in Polynesia*. Seattle: University of Washington Press.

Sauer, C. O. 1952. *Agricultural origins and dispersals*. New York: American Geographical Society.

Schmitt, R. C. 1971. New estimates of the pre-censal population of Hawaii. *JPS* 80: 237–43.

Sharp, C. A. 1956a. *Ancient voyagers in the Pacific*. Wellington: Polynesian Society.

—1956b. The prehistory of the New Zealand Maoris: some possibilities. *JPS* 65: 155–60.

—1960. *The discovery of the Pacific Islands*. Oxford: Clarendon Press.

—1963. *Ancient voyagers in Polynesia*. Auckland: Paul's.

Shawcross, F. W. 1964. An archaeological assemblage of Maori combs. *JPS* 73: 382–98.

—1967. An investigation of prehistoric diet and economy on a coastal site at Galatea Bay, New Zealand. *PPS* 33: 107–31.

—1968. The Ngaroto site. *NZAAN* 11: 2–29.

—1970. Ethnographic economics and the study of population in prehistoric New Zealand: viewed through archaeology. *Mankind* 7: 279–91.

—1972. Energy and ecology: thermodynamic models in archaeology, *in* Clarke, D. L. (ed.) *Models in archaeology*, p. 577–622. London: Methuen.

—1975. Some studies of the influence of prehistoric human predation on marine animal population dynamics, *in* Castell R. W. and G. I. Quimby (eds.) *Maritime adaptations of the Pacific*, p. 39–66. The Hague: Mouton.

Shawcross, K. 1967. Fern root and the total scheme of 18th century Maori food production in agricultural areas. *JPS* 76: 330–52.

Shutler, R. and J. C. March 1975. On the dispersal of the Austronesian horticulturalists. *APAO* 10: 81–113.

Simmons, D. R. 1968. Man, moa and the forest. *Trans. Royal Society of New Zealand* 2: 115–27.

—1969. A New Zealand myth. *New Zealand Journal of History* 3: 14–31.

—1973. Suggested periods in South Island prehistory. *RAIM* 10: 1–58.

Simmons, R. T. 1962. Blood group genes in Polynesians and comparisons with other Pacific peoples. *Oceania* 32: 198–210.

SINOTO, Y. H. 1966. A tentative prehistoric cultural sequence in the northern Marquesas Islands, French Polynesia. *JPS* 75: 287–303.

—1968. Sources of New Zealand's Eastern Polynesian culture: evidence of the cloak pin. *APAO* 3: 30–2.

—1970. An archaeologically based assessment of the Marquesas Islands as a dispersal centre in East Polynesia, *in* Green, R. C. and M. Kelly (eds.) 1970: 105–32.

SINOTO, Y. H. and P. C. McCOY 1975. Report on the preliminary excavation of an early habitation site on Huahine, Society Islands. *JSO* 31: 143–86.

SKINNER, H. D. 1923. *The Morioris of the Chatham Islands. BPBMM* 9, no. 1.

—1974. *Comparatively speaking.* Dunedin: University of Otago Press.

SKINNER, H. D. and W. C. BAUCKE 1928. *The Morioris. BPBMM*, no. 5.

SKJÖLSVOLD, A. 1961. The stone statues and quarries of Rano Raraku, *in* Heyerdahl T. and E. N. Ferdon (eds.) 1961: 97–108.

SMITH, C. S. 1962. An outline of Easter Island archaeology. *Asian Perspectives* 6: 239–44.

SMITH, S. P. 1898–9. *Hawaiki: the whence of the Maori.* Printed in *JPS* volumes 7–8, 3rd edition published by Whitcombe and Tombs, Wellington, 1910.

SOLHEIM, W. G., II 1968. The Batungan Cave sites, Masbate, Philippines. *Asian and Pacific Archaeology Series* 2: 21–62.

—1970. Northern Thailand, Southeast Asia, and world prehistory. *Asian Perspectives* 13: 145–57.

STERNDALE, H. B. 1874. *Memoranda . . . on some of the South Sea Islands.* Appendix to House of Representatives, A. 3B. Wellington: Government Printer.

SUGGS, R. C. 1960. *The island civilisations of Polynesia.* New York: Mentor.

—1961. *The archaeology of Nuku Hiva, Marquesas Islands, French Polynesia.* Papers of the American Museum of Natural History 49, part. 1.

SULLIVAN, A. 1974. Scoria mounds at Wiri. *NZAAN* 17: 128–43.

SUMMERS, C. 1964. *Hawaiian archaeology: fishponds BPBMSP* 52.

THOMAS, W. L. 1967. The Pacific Basin: an introduction, *in* Friis, H. R. (ed.) *The Pacific Basin: a history of its geographic exploration*, p. 1–17. New York: American Geographical Society.

TROTTER, M. M. (ed.) 1974. *Prehistory of the southern Cook Islands.* Canterbury Museum Bulletin 6.

TROTTER, M. M. and B. McCULLOCH 1971. *Prehistoric rock art of New Zealand.* Wellington: Reed.

TUGGLE, H. D. and P. B. GRIFFIN 1973. *Lapakahi, Hawaii: Archaeological studies.* Asian and Pacific Archaeology Series 5.

VERIN, P. 1969. *L'ancienne civilisation de Rurutu.* Paris: Office des Recherches Scientifiques et Techniques Outre-Mer, Mémoir 33.

WALSH, D. S. and B. G. BIGGS 1966. *Proto-Polynesian word list I.* Auckland: Linguistic Society of New Zealand.

WASHBURN, W. E. 1967. The intellectual assumptions and consequences of geographical exploration in the Pacific, *in* Friis H. R. (ed.), *The Pacific Basin: a history of its geographical exploration*, p. 321–34. New York: American Geographical Society.

WILKES, O. R. and R. J. SCARLETT 1967. Excavation of a moa-hunter site at the mouth of the Heaphy River. *Records of the Canterbury Museum* 8: 181–212.

WILLIAMS, J. 1838. *A narrative of missionary enterprises in the South Sea Islands.* London: John Snow.

YEN, D. E. 1961. The adaptation of the *kumara* by the New Zealand Maori. *JPS* 70: 338–48.

—1973. The origins of Oceanic agriculture. *APAO* 8: 68–85.

—1974. *The sweet potato in Oceania. BPBMB* 236.

# List of illustrations

## Acknowledgements

The following maps and plans were drawn by Mrs. J. Goodrum of the Department of Prehistory and Anthropology, Australian National University; figures 1, 5, 6, 19, 21, 29, 36, 37, 39, 48, 51, 55, 66, 75, 87, 98, 101, 104, 107. The photographs in figures 4, 10, 30, 42, 46, 47, 54, 59, 63, 65, 67, 68, 69, 70, 71, 72, 73, 76, 77, 78, 79, 80, 81, 84, 85 and 93, are by the author.

174

# Index